THE ELIJAH DOCTRINE

Chronicle_1 – 1st Phase of the Cryptex puzzle

Written by Elijah H. Bennett

The son of Olivia

"REVELATION OF THE SIGN"

The Elijah Doctrine Chronicles is a complete and accurate decoding of the Bible. The scriptures used in the work are of the NIV (New International Version) translation.

© The Elijah Doctrine Chronicles is protected under U.S. copyright laws. This work may not be duplicated, stored, redistributed, or copied for any purpose without the Author consent.

ISBN: 978-0-692-86335-0

INTRODUCTION

For as long as religion has endured through the Ages, unlocking the secrets behind one of the world's most read and revered books *'The Holy Bible'* has been regarded as one of the most puzzling enigmas of all times. Is the Holy Bible truly a book that guides many of believers along the path to understanding true spiritual enlightenment? Or., could it reveal the revelation of a much deeper truth? A truth that would expose the cornerstone of a 13th century old mystery! A mystery that has long been shrouded in the secrecy of a discovered treasure, and the conspiracy surrounding the leaders of the Christian sect to seek and destroy any trace or existence of it that may prove to undermine their power and influence over Christendom.

For many years it is believed the Holy Grail, found in secret by a group of Crusading Knights known as the Knights Templars, had mysteriously vanished from history and became lost to time. Or was it?

It is my conclusion as the Elijah Doctrine will demonstrate through the three Chronicles series that the Knights Templars, led by the renowned grandmaster Hugues De Payens encoded a sacred map within the scriptures of the Holy Bible to conceal the location of the Grail from those who sought to destroy both the Grail and the Templar Order, until the day of the Grail's unveiling, by the one wise enough to unveil it.

As you explore the Elijah Doctrine Chronicles, you will discover the Holy Bible is much more than a book comprised of ancient stories, but rather, a book constructed into three cryptex puzzles that challenges the worthy in mind and wisdom to unlock the location of the Grail by bringing to light the unseen revelations that are encoded within the verses of the scriptures.

Succeed through each of the three challenging phases of the cryptex puzzles and you will discover three treasure pieces to a sacred Grail map. Each treasure piece will represent a corresponding coordinate to the location of a treasured tomb buried within the biblical texts that will in turn reveal the exact location of the Holy Grail kept secured within an ancient forgotten city. A destroyed city, where it has remained, undisturbed within a small village; a village outside of Jerusalem the Bible calls Golgotha (The Place called Skull)'. It is here, in this very place, where the world will stand and bear witness to the true image of the one God that gave rise to the three pillars of religion!

The revelations you are about to uncover in this Chronicle, "The Elijah Doctrine (Revelation of the sign)," will reveal the true meaning behind these words: ***"Who is wise enough to understand this? Who has been instructed by the LORD and can explain it?" – Jeremiah 9:12***

THE INSTRUCTIONS

1ˢᵀ Phase of the cryptex puzzle

(Note: Each scriptural verse represents a revealing clue! Thus, the revelations revealed by them are much like tiny pieces to a revealing puzzle!)

(Note2: There are four phases of the cryptext puzzle buried within the Holy Bible. The four phases consist of challenging tests that must be overcome: The three tests consist of the following: the test of Superstition, the test of Fear, and the test of Ideology. Each of the four phases will be revealed by the revelations uncovered from the base decoder. The base decoder is the blueprint that will enable you to decipher and understand the mysteries of the scriptures. The more revelations you uncover; the more the base decoder will be expanded revealing each phase of the cryptex puzzle. The building block for the base decoder will be displayed by the following symbol (=). This symbol (=) when not used in a mathematic equation will represent a (correspondence too). For example: (x = x) will come to represent the following: (x corresponds to x))

The goal in the 1ˢᵗ phase of the cryptex puzzle is to overcome: **[The test of Superstition]**

Welcome to the Elijah Doctrine!

THE 1ST EXODUS PERIOD

CHAPTER ONE - 1st PHASE OF THE CRYPTEX PUZZLE- REVELATION OF THE SIGN

In this chapter, you must identify a series of hidden clues that will begin to construct the base decoder.

To start, you must look carefully at the following descriptions of Revelation 17:9-11,

> [This calls for a mind with wisdom. **(1) The seven heads are seven hills on which the woman sits. They are also seven kings. (2) Five have fallen, one is, the other has not yet come; but when he does come, he must remain for a little while. (3) The beast who once was, and now is not, is an eighth king. He belongs to the seven and is going to his destruction**]

Next, remove the bold descriptions from the verses in numbered order.

1- [The seven heads are seven hills on which the woman sits. They are also seven kings]

2- [Five have fallen, one is, the other has not yet come; but when he does come, he must remain for a little while]

3- [The beast who once was, and now is not, is an eighth king. He belongs to the seven and is going to this destruction]

(Note: The following three descriptions including a fourth (not shown in this illustration but will be revealed moving forward) are four tests that must be understood to complete the 1st phase of the cryptex puzzle)

To begin, you must solve the mystery concealed behind the [**1st test**]:

[The seven heads are seven hills on which the woman sits. They are also seven kings]

(Note2: There is an important revelation missing from this description. For example: Within this description reveals a hidden clue)

*(Note3: To solve this mystery, you must start by revealing the hidden revelations concealed behind the mystery regarding the following seven horns: (**two-horned** ram), (**large horned** goat) and (**four-horns** that replaced the goat's large horn). Each horn reveals a separate revelation that must be understood to advance the understanding into the mysteries of their symbolic meaning)*

To start, you must look carefully at the bold portion in the following description of Daniel 8:3.

> [**Daniel has a vision, in which he saw a two-horned ram standing beside the canal.** One of the horns was longer than the other, but grew up later]

(Note4: The two-horned ram in this description is symbolic and reveals a very important revelation)

To understand the mystery of this, you must begin by looking closely at the description in the verse of Revelation 13:11.

> [Then I saw another beast, coming out of the earth. He had two horns like a lamb, but he spoke like a dragon]

*(Note5: Within this verse reveals the hidden clue. For example: The word 'lamb' is symbolic and represents a young sheep. Thus, a two-horned beast, with two horns like a lamb, is also symbolic for what is called a male two-horned sheep, otherwise known as a **<u>two-horned ram</u>**)*

Here is the revelation. The two-horned ram as corresponding to the 'beast coming out of the earth' represents the rise of the following era: [The Ram Age].

(Note6: Though the Ram is symbolic for representing "The Ram Age," its two horns are also symbolic and reveal two separate revelations apart from the Ram itself)

Next, return to the description of Daniel 8:3 and look closely at the bold description.

> [Daniel has a vision, in which he saw a two-horned ram standing beside the canal. **One of the horns was longer than the other, but grew up later**]

To understand the mystery of this you must locate another hidden clue found in the book of Judges 2:10.

> [**After that whole generation had been gathered to their fathers another generation grew up**, who knew neither the Lord nor what he had done for Israel]

If you look closely at this description, you will discover that the ram's longer horn corresponds to the description *'After that whole generation had been gathered to their fathers'*. This generation of Israelites corresponds to the Israelites who according to the scriptures exited from the land of Egypt. This generation will come to represent the Elder Generation as revealed by the illustration below,

- {Longer horn} = [*After that whole generation had been gathered to their fathers* = **Elder Generation**]

Also, within this description, you will discover that the ram's short horn, which grew up later, corresponds to the second part of this description *'another generation grew up'*. This generation of Israelites corresponds to the Israelites who according to the scriptures crossed over into the land of Canaan. This generation will come to represent the Descendant Generation as revealed by the illustration below,

- {Short horn} = [***another generation grew up*** = **Descendent Generation**]

These two horns corresponding to two generations also represent two exodus periods that will mark the beginning and end periods for the Age of Ram.

(Note 7: The 1ˢᵗ exodus period corresponds to the elder generation of Israelites exiled from the land of Egypt. The 2ⁿᵈ exodus period corresponds to the descendant generation of Israelites exiled to two different lands that will be ruled by two different Empires. The names of these two Empires will be revealed later as we uncover more revelations)

Now, merge the revelations together to illustrate what has been uncovered.

For example: The two-horned ram, known as the *'beast coming out of the earth'* corresponds to the emergence of the Ram Age.

- The Two-Horned Ram *('beast coming out of the earth')* = Ram Age

Its larger horn represents the start of the Ram Age which will begin during the 1ˢᵗ Exodus period. Thus, it is the exodus of the elder generation that will mark the Beginning timeline corresponding to the Ram Age.

- {Longer horn} = [**Start of the Ram Age = 1ˢᵗ Exodus period** *(Beginning Timeline marker)* = **Exodus from the land of Egypt** = Elder generation = *After that whole generation had been gathered to their fathers*]

The short horn, which grew up later, represents the end of the Ram Age which will end during the 2ⁿᵈ Exodus period. Thus, it is the exile of the descendent generation that will mark the ending timeline corresponding to the Ram Age.

- {Shorter horn} = [**End of the Ram Age = 2ⁿᵈ Exodus period** *(Ending Timeline marker)* = **Exiled to the lands of (?)_(?)** = Descendent generation = *another generation grew up*]

These two horns will also come to represent the first two nations born in the Ram Age.

To understand this, we will need to locate another set of clues found in the verses of Exodus 32:5 and 1st Kings 12:38. Look closely at the bold descriptions.

- Exodus 32:5 – [When Aaron saw this, **he built an altar in front of the calf** and announced, "Tomorrow there will be a festival to the Lord"]

- 1st Kings 12:28 – [After seeking advice, **the king made two golden calves**]

The word 'Calf' in the description of Exodus is symbolic and represents an adult bull. Thus, it symbolic for representing the Elder generation.

- {Longer horn} = [Elder generation = *After that whole generation had been gathered to their fathers* = **Golden Calf (?)**]

The words 'golden calves' in the description of 1st Kings is also symbolic and represents the offspring from the adult bull. Thus, they are symbolic for representing the Descendent generation.

- {Shorter horn} = [Descendent generation = *another generation grew up* = **Golden Calves (?)**]

The golden Calf and the golden calves corresponding to the longer and short horns are also symbolic and represent two nations that will emerge in the Ram Age. To reveal the mystery behind them you must locate another clue in the verse of 1st Chronicles 1:28.

Look closely at the description below,

[The sons of Abraham: Isaac and Ishmael]

If you look closely at this description, you will discover that Ishmael, elder son born to Abraham, represents the Nation of Ishmael and corresponds to the longer horn as representing the elder generation. Thus, the golden Calf represents the descendants Ishmael as revealed by the illustration below,

- [Longer horn] = **{Nation of Ishmael} = {Father of the 1st kingdom born in the Ram's Age}** = [Elder generation = *After that whole generation had been gathered to their fathers*] = **[Golden Calf (descendants of Ishmael)]** = [Start of the Ram Age = 1st Exodus period *(Beginning Timeline marker)*] = [Exodus from the land of Egypt]

(Note8: Ishmael, as corresponding to the elder generation will come to represent the father of the first kingdom born in the Ram Age. It is from this kingdom where the nations of Isaac will emerge. This revelation corresponds to the verse of Genesis 21:17-18 - **'God heard the boy crying, and the angel of God called to Hagar from heaven and said to her, "What is the matter, Hagar? Do not be afraid; God has heard the boy crying as he lies there. Lift the boy up and take him by the hand. For I will make him into a great nation"'.** *This revelation will be revealed in more detail moving forward)*

You will also discover that Isaac, the second born son of Abraham, represents the Nation of Isaac and corresponds to the short horn which grew up later as representing the descendent generation. Thus, the golden Calves represents the descendants of Isaac as revealed by the illustration below,

- [Short horn] = **{Nation of Isaac} = {Father of the first two nations born out of the 1st kingdom}** = [Descendent generation = *another generation grew up*] = **[Golden Calves (descendants of Isaac)]** = [Exiled to the land of (?)_(?)] = [End of the Ram Age *(Ending Timeline marker)*]

(Note9: Isaac, as corresponding to the descendent generation will come to represent the father of two nations that will emerge from the nation of Ishmael, before emerging into their own kingdoms. Thus, these two descendent nations will come to represent the first two nations born from the 1st kingdom. This revelation corresponds to the following description in the verse of Genesis 17:19 - **'Then God said, "Yes, but your wife Sarah will bear you a son, and you will call him Isaac. I will establish my covenant with him as an everlasting covenant for his descendants after him.'** *This revelation will also be revealed in more detail moving forward)*

Next, let's look closer at the description in the verse of Daniel 8:20.

[The two-horned ram that you saw represents the kings of Media and Persia]

If you look closely at this description, you will discover it is structurally written deceptively.

For example: Media and Persia are symbolic and serve only as a revealing clue that helps to identify the mystery of the two horns. They do not, however, represent the two horns.

To understand this, you must merge the ram's two-horns revealed in Daniel Chapter 8:20 with the description in the verse of Revelation 17:9.

Here, you will discover that the two-horns correspond to two heads that are two hills on which the woman sits. This revelation reveals the two horns to represent two kings as revealed by the illustration below,

- **{Two horns}** = [two heads = two hills = two kings]

THE GOAT

The next thing you must do is look carefully at the bold portion in the following description of Daniel 8:5-7.

> [As I was thinking about this, **suddenly a goat with a prominent horn between his eyes came from the west**, crossing the whole earth without touching the ground. He came toward the two horned ram I had seen standing beside the canal and charged at him in great rage]

(Note11: This description reveals two vital clues. For example: The goat in this description is symbolic and bears a different symbolic meaning apart from its large horn. The first clue is revealed in the following two descriptions of Genesis and Daniel)

Look closely at the following bold portions in the descriptions below,

- Genesis 22:13 - [**Abraham saw in a thicket**, a ram caught by its horns. **He took the ram and sacrificed it** instead of his son]

- Daniel 8:7 – [I saw him attack the ram furiously, striking the ram and shattering his two horns. **The ram was powerless to stand against him; the goat knocked him to the ground and trampled on him**, and none could rescue the ram from his power]

(Note12: If you examine the two verses you will notice that Abraham as described in the bold description of Genesis 22:13 corresponds to the goat as described in the description of Daniel 8:7))

(Note13: If you examine the bold verses in the description below, you will notice that the two-horned ram corresponds to Abraham's descendants Ishmael and Isaac as representing the longer horn and the short horn which grew up later))

- Genesis 22:13 - [Abraham saw in a thicket, **a ram caught by its horns**. He took the ram and sacrificed it instead of his son]

- Daniel 8:7 – [I saw him attack the ram furiously, **striking the ram and shattering his two horns. The ram was powerless to stand against him**; the goat knocked him to the ground and trampled on him, and none could rescue the ram from his power]

Here is the next clue: Abraham *(father of Ishmael and Isaac)* corresponds to the 'goat' *(the elder of ram)* and represents the following revelation: [**trampled on ram**].

Ishmael and Isaac *(sons of Abraham)* correspond to the 'two-horned ram' *(descendant of goat)* and represents the following revelation: [**sacrificed ram**]

Here is the [**1st vital clue**]: Abraham corresponds to the goat, who shatters the ram's two horns as representing the Nation of Ishmael and the Nation of Isaac and represent the Father of the Ram Age

This revelation is revealed by the illustration below:

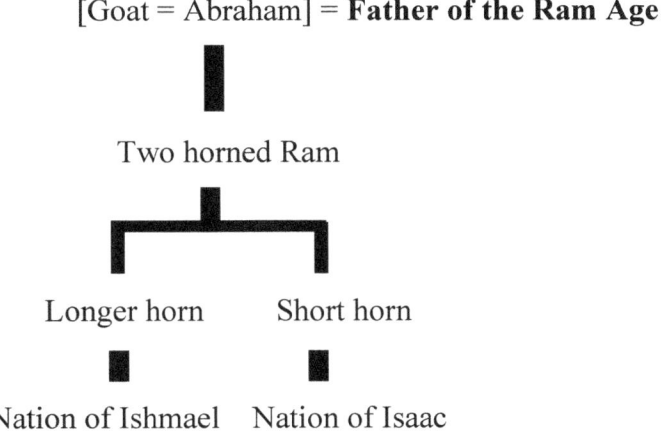

(Note14: This revelation reveals the meaning behind this description 'He took him outside and said, "Look up at the sky and count the stars- if indeed you can count them." Then he said to him, "So shall your offspring be" – Genesis 15:5.)

(Note15: The second vital clue is revealed by understanding the symbolic meaning of what the goat's large horn represents)

The Goat's LONG-HORN

The next thing you must do is look closely at the following description of Daniel 8:21.

[The shaggy goat represent the king of Greece, the large horn between its eyes is the first king]

(Note16: This description is also structured deceptively and reveals another vital clue! To reveal the clue, you must merge the goat's (large horn) with the description of Revelation 17:9. For example: The goat's large horn corresponds to a third head that is a third hill on which the woman sits)

Here is the [2nd vital clue]: The **goat's large horn** corresponds to a **third head that is a third hill**, on which the woman sits and represents the following revelation: [a **third king**]

The next thing you must do is merge the revelations together in the correct places.

- **{Large horn}** = [3rd head = 3rd hill = 3rd king]

(Note17: Abraham (shaggy goat) does not represent a 3rd king (nor does he represent the king of Greece). As revealed previously, the shaggy goat is symbolic and corresponds to Abraham as representing the Father of the Ram Age. The large horn, however, represents a 3rd king and reveals a separate revelation apart from the goat. This revelation will be revealed in more detail moving forward)

(Note18: There is another vital clue regarding the goat. For example: Four more horns will emerge from the goat to replace the large horn, which fell reaching the height of its power. This clue is also revealed in the description of Daniel)

THE FOUR PROMINENT HORNS

The next thing you must do is look closely at the bold portion in the description of Daniel 8:8.

> **[Daniel noticed four prominent horns rise to replace the goat's large horn**, which broke reaching the height of its power]

(Note19: To reveal the vital clue, you must also merge the goat's (four prominent horns) with the description of Revelation 17:9. For example: The four prominent horns correspond to a 4th, 5th, 6th and 7th head that is a 4th, 5th, 6th and 7th hill, on which the woman sits)

Here is the next [vital clue]: The **four prominent horns** correspond to a **4th, 5th, 6th and 7th head** that is a **4th, 5th, 6th and 7th hill**, on which the woman sits, and represents the following: [**4th, 5th, 6th and 7th king**].

The next thing you must do is merge the revelations together in the correct places.

- {1^{ST} prominent horn} = [4TH **head** = 4TH **hill** = 4TH **king**]

- {2^{ND} prominent horn} = [5TH **head** = 5TH **hill** = 5TH **king**]

- {3^{RD} prominent horn} = [6TH **head** = 6TH **hill** = 6TH **king**]

- {4^{TH} prominent horn} = [7TH **head** = 7TH **hill** = 7TH **king**]

(Note20: There is another vital clue regarding the four prominent horns. To locate this clue, look closely at the description of Daniel)

Look closely at the bold portion in the following description of Daniel 8:22 below,

> **[The four horns that replaced the one that was broken off represent four kingdoms** that will emerge from his nation but will not have the same power]

(Note21: To reveal this clue, you must merge the (four kingdoms) with the four prominent horns (that replaced the large horn that was broken))

Here is the next [vital clue]: The 1st, 2nd, 3rd and 4th prominent horns also represent the following kingdoms: [1st, 2nd, 3rd and 4th kingdoms].

The next thing you must do is merge the revelations together in the correct places.

- $\{1^{ST}$ prominent horn$\}$ = [4TH head = 4TH hill = 4TH king] = **[1st kingdom]**

- $\{2^{ND}$ prominent horn$\}$ = [5TH head = 5TH hill = 5TH king] = **[2nd kingdom]**

- $\{3^{RD}$ prominent horn$\}$ = [6TH head = 6TH hill = 6TH king] = **[3rd kingdom]**

- $\{4^{TH}$ prominent horn$\}$ = [7TH head = 7TH hill = 7TH king] = **[4th kingdom]**

(Note22: There is also another vital clue regarding the four kingdoms. To locate this clue, look again at the description of Daniel)

Look closely at the bold portion in the following description of Daniel 7:17 below,

[The **four great beasts are four kingdoms** that will rise from the earth]

(Note23: To reveal this clue, you must merge the (four great beasts) with the four kingdoms (that are also four prominent horns))

Here is the next **[vital clue]**: The 1st, 2nd, 3rd and 4th kingdoms also correspond to the following four beasts: [1st, 2nd, 3rd and 4th great beasts].

The next thing you must do is merge the revelations together in the correct places.

- {1ST prominent horn} = [4TH head = 4TH hill = 4TH king] = **[1ST beast = 1ST kingdom]**

- {2ND prominent horn} = [5TH head = 5TH hill = 5TH king] = **[2ND beast = 2ND kingdom]**

- {3RD prominent horn} = [6TH head = 6TH hill = 6TH king] = **[3RD beast = 3RD kingdom]**

- {4TH prominent horn} = [7TH head = 7TH hill = 7TH king] = **[4TH beast = 4TH kingdom]**

(Note24: To reveal the base decoder merge the entire revelations regarding the two-horn (ram), large horn (goat) and the four prominent horns (goat), together into the correct context to reflex their respective kings)

THE BASE DECODER

- **{Two horns}** = [two heads = two hills = two kings]

- **{Large horn}** = [3RD head = 3RD hill = 3RD king]

- **{1^{ST} prominent horn}** = [4TH head = 4TH hill = 4TH king] = [1ST beast = 1ST kingdom]

- **{2^{ND} prominent horn}** = [5TH head = 5TH hill = 5TH king] = [2ND beast = 2ND kingdom]

- **{3^{RD} prominent horn}** = [6TH head = 6TH hill = 6TH king] = [3RD beast = 3RD kingdom]

- **{4^{TH} prominent horn}** = [7TH head = 7TH hill = 7TH king] = [4TH beast = 4TH kingdom]

*(Note25: This revelation reveals the meaning behind the description of Revelation 17:9 - 'This calls for a mind with wisdom. The **(seven horns)** are seven heads and seven hills on which the woman sits. They are also seven kings!')*

(Note26: You must use the base decoder to navigate the scriptures to complete the 2nd, 3rd, and 4th chapters! The base decoder will be expanded as more revelations are revealed)

Congratulations! You have successfully completed the [1st test]!

The next thing you must do is solve the mystery concealed behind the **[2nd test]**.

[Five have fallen, one is, the other has not yet come; but when he does come, he must remain for a little while]

(Note: To solve this mystery you must dig deeper into the revelation regarding the seven horns!)

The first thing you must do is look carefully at the bold portion in description of Daniel 7:2-3 below,

[In my vision at night I looked, and there before me were the four winds of heaven churning up the great sea. **Four great beasts, each different from the others, came up out of the sea**]

Look closely at the identity of the following beasts as seen below,

- $\{1^{ST}$ prominent horn$\} = [4^{TH}$ head $= 4^{TH}$ hill $= 4^{TH}$ king$] = [1^{ST}$ beast $=$ **lion** $= 1^{ST}$ kingdom$]$

- $\{2^{ND}$ prominent horn$\} = [5^{TH}$ head $= 5^{TH}$ hill $= 5^{TH}$ king$] = [2^{ND}$ beast $=$ **bear** $= 2^{ND}$ kingdom$]$

- $\{3^{RD}$ prominent horn$\} = [6^{TH}$ head $= 6^{TH}$ hill $= 6^{TH}$ king$] = [3^{RD}$ beast $=$ **leopard** $= 3^{RD}$ kingdom$]$

- $\{4^{TH}$ prominent horn$\} = [7^{TH}$ head $= 7^{TH}$ hill $= 7^{TH}$ king$] = [4^{TH}$ beast $= (?) = 4^{TH}$ kingdom$]$

(Note2: If you look closely, you will discover the identity of the 4TH beast is missing. The description of Daniel 7:2-3 reveals two vital clues. For example: The 4th beast reveals a great revelation. To locate the clues, you must start by looking closely at the description of Daniel)

THE FOURTH BEAST and the TEN HORNS

Look closely at the bold portions in the description of Daniel 3:7 below,

[After that, in my vision at night I looked, and **there before me was a fourth beast-terrifying and frightening and very powerful**. It had large iron teeth; it crushed and devoured its victims and was different from all the former beasts, **and it had ten horns**]

*(Note3: The first clue is revealed behind the symbolic meaning of what the **beast** represents. The second clue is revealed behind the symbolic meaning of what the **ten horns** represent (thus, both reveal separate revelations). However, it is only when the **(beast)** and the **(ten horns)** are unified will they represent what Daniel describes as a fourth beast with ten horns. This revelation will be revealed in more detail shortly)*

THE TEN HORNS

The first thing you must do is look closely at the bold portion in the following description of Revelation 17:12.

> [**The ten horns you saw are ten kings who have not yet received a kingdom**, but who for one hour will receive authority as kings along with the beast]

Here is the next clue: The ten horns correspond to the following revelation: [ten kings who have not yet received a kingdom].

(Note4: These ten kings correspond to the ten horns that rest on the 4th beast's head))

*(Note5: There is also an important revelation revealed behind the following description 'who have not yet received a kingdom.' This revelation will be revealed in detail very shortly! To locate the first vital clue regarding the **4th beast** and the **ten horns**, you must start by solving the mystery in the description of Daniel 2:41)*

Look closely at the following description of Daniel 2:41 below,

> [Just as you saw that the feet and toes were partly of baked clay and partly of iron, so this will be a divided kingdom, yet it will have some of the strength of iron in it, even as you saw iron mixed with clay]

(Note6: To solve this mystery, you must reveal a set of multiple clues hidden within the biblical account of how King David and King Solomon came to power)

KING DAVID and KING SOLOMON

King David conquered a fortress City, once ruled by the Jebusites *(2nd Samuel 5:7)*. After taking possession of the Kingdom, King David brought together the tribes of Israel and united them under the Kingdom re-named in his honor, the City of David *(2nd Samuel 5:9)*.

(Note7: The following tribes correspond to the descendants of Jacob; for Jacob produced twelve descendants. The name Israel, according to the account, foretelling a wrestling match between Jacob and a mystery man, derives from the man having rewarded Jacob with a new name. Thus, the name Jacob becomes transformative to which he would later become known symbolically as Israel. His descendants (called Israelites) would adopt the phrase 'the tribes of Israel.'))

After becoming King over Israel, King David performed great wonders unto his God, winning many battles and conquering many nations, he expanded the City of David throughout the land, giving each tribe, descending from Jacob, their own territory in the land.

By the time of his death, his son Solomon succeeds him as King and becomes king over Israel establishing his throne as ruler throughout the City of David. Thus, King Solomon built the great Temple of the Lord.

Now King Solomon enjoyed a time of great prosperity and peace and so he grew in wisdom and in wealth. Before his death, the God of David would send a messenger to Egypt to seek out a former official of King Solomon who fled to Egypt before Solomon's death. The man's name is Jeroboam, an Ephraimite from Zeredah *(1st Kings 11:26)*.

The massager foretold a revelation to Jeroboam detailing how the Kingdom would be torn apart from King Solomon's rule and divided *(1st Kings 11:34)*.

The messenger revealed to Jeroboam how he would receive ten tribes of the Kingdom *(1st Kings 11:31)*, to which, one tribe would remain in the city to serve as a burning lamp before the God of David *(1st Kings 11:36)*.

Here is the next clue: The **ten horns** correspond to **ten kings** and represent the following revelation: [ten tribes].

*(Note8: These ten tribes of the kingdom have been allotted to Jeroboam. These **ten tribes** also correspond to the following description '**who are yet to receive a kingdom of their own!**' This revelation will be revealed in more detail moving forward!)*

Here is the next clue: The **4th beast** represents the following revelation: [single tribe].

*(Note9: The **4th beast** (apart from its ten horns) corresponds to the **single tribe** that will remain in the city. This revelation will be revealed in more detail moving forward!))*

Here is the [1st vital clue]: The following description of Daniel 2:41: **'Just as you saw that the feet and toes were partly of baked clay and partly of iron, so this will be a divided kingdom, yet it will have some of the strength of iron in it, even as you saw iron mixed with clay'** represents the following revelation: [A divided 4th kingdom].

*(Note10: As previously revealed, the 4th beast with ten horns represents a 4th kingdom. Thus, the eleven tribes in total make up the 4th kingdom. As revealed, the kingdom is being torn apart and will be divided. Therefore, If you examine this description **'yet it will have some of the strength of iron in it, even as you saw iron mixed with clay'** you will discover it corresponds to the bold description in the verse of 1st Kings 11:34 – **'But I will not take the whole kingdom out of Solomon's hand; I have made him ruler all the days of his life for the sake of David my servant, whom I chose and who obeyed my commands and decrees.'** - This revelation will also be revealed in more detail moving forward!)*

The next thing you must do is divide the [4th beast] apart from its [ten horns] to reflect a divided 4th kingdom and merge the revelations together into the correct places.

- {Ten Horns} = [Ten kings = **Ten tribes** = *who are yet to receive a kingdom of their own*]

- {Beast} = [**single tribe** = *remained in the city*]

(Note11: This revelation also reveals another hidden clue. For example: Within the description of 1st Kings 11:36, the name of this city, will reveal the name of the 4th kingdom)

Here is the **[2nd vital clue]:** The name of the 4th kingdom is: **The City of David!**

(Note12: The name of the 4th Kingdom (City of David) does not reflect the symbolic name hidden behind the 4th beast (though the 4th beast represents a 4th kingdom). The fourth beast is also symbolic and reveals a separate revelation that will be revealed in detail in the later chapters!)

The next thing you must do is bring back the revelation revealed by the base decoder and merge the revelations together into the correct place.

{4TH prominent horn} = [7TH head = 7TH hill = 7TH king] = [4TH beast (ten horns)] = [4TH kingdom = Divided Kingdom = **City of David**:

- {Ten Horns} = [Ten kings = Ten tribes = *who are yet to receive a kingdom of their own*]

- {Beast} = [single tribe = *remained in the city*]

(Note13: To locate the next vital clue regarding the beast and the ten horns, you must solve the mystery revealed by Daniel 2:42)

Look closely at the following description of Daniel 2:42 below,

[As the toes were partly iron and partly clay, so this kingdom will be partly strong and partly brittle. And just as you saw the iron mixed with baked clay, so the people will be a mixture and will not remain united, anymore than iron mixes with clay]

(Note14: To solve this mystery, you must continue along the biblical account proceeding after the death of King Solomon. Within the description of 1st Kings 14:21 reveals another clue. The revelation revealed by this clue will reveal the mystery regarding the divide of the Fourth kingdom)

A.D. OF KING SOLOMON

After the death of King Solomon, he was succeeded by his son, Rehoboam *(1st Kings 14:21)*!

*(Note15: The beast which corresponds to a single tribe represents the tribe allotted to Rehoboam (Solomon's son). This **single tribe** also corresponds to the following description **'I will give one tribe to his son so that David my servant may always have a lamp before me in Jerusalem, the city where I chose to put my Name'** – 1st Kings 11:36. This revelation will also be revealed in more detail moving forward!)*

Next, bring back the revelations and merge the kings in their proper places corresponding to their allotment.

$\{4^{TH}$ prominent horn$\} = [7^{TH}$ head $= 7^{TH}$ hill $= 7^{TH}$ king$] = [4^{TH}$ beast (ten horns)$] = [4^{TH}$ kingdom $=$ Divided Kingdom $=$ City of David:

- $\{$Ten Horns$\} = [$Ten kings $=$ Ten tribes $= $ *who are yet to receive a kingdom of their own* $= $ **King Jeroboam**]

- $\{$Beast$\} = [$single tribe $= $ *remained in the city* $= $ **King Rehoboam**]

The next thing you must do is look carefully at the following description of 1st Kings 11:34-36.

[But I will take the whole kingdom out of Solomon's hand; I have made him ruler all the days of his life for the sake of David my servant, whom I chose and who observed my commands and statutes. **I will take the kingdom from his son's hands and give you ten tribes. I will give one tribe to his son** so that David my servant may always have a lamp before me in Jerusalem, the city where I chose to put my name]

Next, remove the bold description from the verses and merge them with the previous revelations regarding the divide of the 4th kingdom into the correct places.

{4TH prominent horn} = [7TH head = 7TH hill = 7TH king] = [4TH beast (ten horns)] = [4TH kingdom = Divided Kingdom = City of David:

- {Ten Horns} = [Ten kings = Ten tribes = ***I will take the kingdom from his son's hands and give you ten tribes*** = King Jeroboam = *who are yet to receive a kingdom of their own*]

- {Beast} = [single tribe = ***I will give one tribe to his son*** = King Rehoboam = *remained in the city*]

Next, look closely at the description in the verses of Revelation 7:5-8, as seen below,

1. [From the tribes of *Judah* 12,000 were sealed]
2. [From the tribes of *Reuben* 12,000 were sealed]
3. [From the tribes of *Gad* 12,000 were sealed]
4. [From the tribes of *Asher* 12,000 were sealed]
5. [From the tribes of *Naphtali* 12,000 were sealed]
6. [From the tribes of *Manasseh* 12,000 were sealed]
7. [From the tribe of *Simeon* 12,000 were sealed]
8. [From the tribe of *Levi* 12,000 were sealed]
9. [From the tribe of *Issachar* 12,000 were sealed]
10. [From the tribe of *Zebulon* 12,000 were sealed]
11. [From the tribe of *Joseph* 12,000 were sealed]
12. [From the tribe of *Benjamin* 12,000 were sealed]

(Note16: One of the names listed among the twelve tribes does not represent a tribe. The name of this tribe represents a nation that is born from one of the eleven tribes. Thus, one of these two kings will become king over this nation!)

Next, look again at the description in the verses of Revelation 7:5-8 and remove the tribe of Judah from the verses as seen below,

1- [From the tribes of *Reuben* 12,000 were sealed]
2- [From the tribes of *Gad* 12,000 were sealed]
3- [From the tribes of *Asher* 12,000 were sealed]
4- [From the tribes of *Naphtali* 12,000 were sealed]
5- [From the tribes of *Manasseh* 12,000 were sealed]
6- [From the tribe of *Simeon* 12,000 were sealed]
7- [From the tribe of *Levi* 12,000 were sealed]
8- [From the tribe of *Issachar* 12,000 were sealed]
9- [From the tribe of *Zebulon* 12,000 were sealed]
10- [From the tribe of *Joseph* 12,000 were sealed]
11- [From the tribe of *Benjamin* 12,000 were sealed]

*(Note17: The name **'Judah'** is symbolic and does not represent a tribe (nor does Judah represent a child born to Jacob). This revelation will be revealed in more detail shortly as well as moving forward))*

The next thing you must do is merge the following tribes allotted to their respective kings with the revelations revealed by the divide of the 4th kingdom into the correct places.

{4TH prominent horn} = [7TH head = 7TH hill = 7TH king] = [4TH beast (ten horns)] = [4TH kingdom = Divided Kingdom = City of David:

- {Ten Horns} = [Ten kings = Ten tribes = *I will take the kingdom from his son's hands and give you ten tribes* = **Tribes of Ephraim, Manasseh, Naphtali, Dan, Asher, Issachar, Zebulon, Simeon, Reuben, and Gad** = King Jeroboam = *who are yet to receive a kingdom of their own*]

- {Beast} = [single tribe = *I will give one tribe to his son* = **Tribe of Benjamin** = *remained in the city* = King Rehoboam]

*(Note18: The **tribe of Judah** is symbolic and represents the name of a nation, known as the **Nation of Judah**. The Nation of Judah emerges from the tribe of Benjamin (thus, the tribe of Benjamin would move on to forge its own nation). Therefore, the Kingdom formally known as the City of David will no longer be called the City of David, but rather, the Nation of Judah (thus, Rehoboam will become king of this nation))*

Next, merge the nation of Judah with the revelations regarding the divide of the 4th kingdom into the correct places.

{4^{TH} prominent horn} = [7TH head = 7TH hill = 7TH king] = [4TH beast (ten horns)] = [4TH kingdom = Divided Kingdom = City of David:

- {Ten Horns} = [Ten kings = Ten tribes = *I will take the kingdom from his son's hands and give you ten tribes* = Tribes of: Ephraim, Manasseh, Naphtali, Dan, Asher, Issachar, Zebulon, Simeon, Reuben, and Gad = King Jeroboam = *who are yet to receive a kingdom of their own*]

- {Beast} = [single tribe = *I will give one tribe to his son* = Tribe of Benjamin = *remained in the city* = **Nation of Judah = Rehoboam king of Judah**]

*(Note19: There is also a hidden clue regarding Jeroboam. This clue will begin to shed light on the meaning behind the bold part of this description 'The ten horns you saw are ten kings **who have not yet received a kingdom of its own**' – Revelation 17:12. The clue is revealed in the description of 1st Kings)*

Look closely at the bold portion in the following description of 1st Kings 12:15 below,

[Then **Jeroboam fortified Shechem in the hill country of Ephraim** and lived there]

*(Note20: The **hill country of Ephraim** corresponds to the land of Israel (Thus, Jeroboam is called an Ephraimite from Zeredah' - 1st Kings 11:26). Also, Jeroboam as revealed throughout the books of Kings and Chronicles will become the king of Israel. This nation corresponds to the following description 'The ten horns you saw are ten kings who have not yet received a kingdom' – Revelation 17:12)*

Here is the next clue: The ten tribes allotted to Jeroboam will emerge into the following nation: [Nation of Ephraim *(also known as the land of Israel)*].

Next, merge the nation of Ephraim with the revelations regarding the divide of the 4th kingdom into the correct place.

{4TH prominent horn} = [7TH head = 7TH hill = 7TH king] = [4TH beast (ten horns)] = [4TH kingdom = Divided Kingdom = City of David:

> {Ten Horns} = [Ten kings = Ten tribes = *I will take the kingdom from his son's hands and give you ten tribes* = Tribes of: Ephraim, Manasseh, Naphtali, Dan, Asher, Issachar, Zebulon, Simeon, Reuben, and Gad = Jeroboam king of Ephraim = **Nation of Ephraim (land of Israel)** = *who are yet to receive a kingdom of their own*]

- {Beast} = [single tribe = *I will give one tribe to his son* = Tribe of Benjamin = *remained in the city* = Nation of Judah = Rehoboam king of Judah]

*(Note21: These two nations **Ephraim** (land of Israel) and **Judah** will come to represent the first two nations born out of the 1st Kingdom (revealed as the City of David). These two nations will descend from the Nation of Isaac. This revelation will be revealed in more detail shortly. The two nations: Ephraim (the land of Israel), and Judah, will materialize into neighboring enemies, and as a people, united by King David and presided over by King Solomon will no longer remained unified as a Kingdom (City of David))*

Here is the next **[vital clue]**: The following description of Daniel 2:42: '**As the toes were partly iron and partly clay, so this kingdom will be partly strong and partly brittle. And just as you saw the iron mixed with baked clay, so the people will be a mixture and will not remain united, anymore than iron mixes with clay**' corresponds to the divide of the 4th kingdom and represents the following revelation revealed by the description of Isaiah 7:17: [Ephraim *(the land of Israel)*, broke away from Judah].

The next thing you must do is bring back the following revelation revealed by the Longer horn and short horn regarding the nations of Ishmael and Isaac.

- [Longer horn] = {Nation of Ishmael} = {Father of the 1st kingdom born in the Ram's Age} = [Elder generation = *After that whole generation had been gathered to their fathers*] = [Golden Calf *(descendants of Ishmael)*] = [Start of the Ram Age = 1st Exodus period *(Beginning Timeline marker)*] = [Exodus from the land of Egypt]

- [Short horn] = {Nation of Isaac} = {Father of the first two nations born out of the 1st kingdom} = [Descendent generation = *another generation grew up*] = [Golden Calves *(descendants of Isaac)*] = [Exiled to the land of (?)_(?)] = [End of the Ram Age *(Ending Timeline marker)*]

Here, you must merge the revelations revealed by the translation of Daniel's 1st and 2nd visions in their respective places. There are four vital clues that must be revealed to achieve this.

Here is the **[1st vital clue]**: The Golden Calf (as representing the word elder) corresponds to the elder generation (longer horn) and represents the 1st Kingdom born in the Ram Age: [The City of David].

*(Note23: **Ishmael** (elder son of Abraham) will come to represent the father of the 1st Kingdom born in the Ram Age, the City of David. This revelation reveals the meaning behind the verses of Genesis 21:17-18 - 'God heard the boy crying, and the angel of God called to Hagar from heaven and said to her, "What is the matter, Hagar? Do not be afraid; God has heard the boy crying as he lies there. Lift the boy up and take him by the hand. For I will make him into a great nation"')*

(Note24: It is from this Kingdom, where the eleven tribes representing the following two nations: The Nation of Ephraim (ten tribes) and the Nation of Judah (single tribe), will emerge from))

The next thing you must do is bring back the following revelation revealed by the [Longer horn] and merge the revelation together regarding the nation of Ishmael in its proper place.

- [Longer horn] = {Nation of Ishmael} = {Father of the 1st kingdom born in the Ram's Age = **The City of David *(first Kingdom born in the Ram Age)*** } = [Elder generation = *After that whole generation had been gathered to their fathers*] = [Golden Calf *(descendants of Ishmael)*] = [Start of the Ram Age = 1st Exodus period *(Beginning Timeline marker)*] = [Exodus from the land of Egypt]

Here is the **[2nd vital clue]**: The Golden Calves (as representing the word offspring) corresponds to the descendant generation (short horn) and represents the following two nations born out of the City of David as representing a divided Kingdom: [The Nation of Ephraim *(land of Israel)* and The Nation of Judah]!

*(Note25: **Isaac** (second born son of Abraham) will come to represent the father of these two nations: the nation of Judah and the Nation of Ephraim, both of which will emerge from the City of David as representing a divided kingdom. This revelation reveals the meaning behind the verse of Genesis 17:19 - 'Then God said, "Yes, but your wife Sarah will bear you a son, and you will call him Isaac. I will establish my covenant with him as an everlasting covenant for his descendants after him.'))*

The next thing you must do is bring back the following revelation revealed by the [Short horn] and merge the revelation together regarding the nation of Isaac in its proper places.

- [Short horn] = {Nation of Isaac} = {Father of the first two nations born out of the 1st kingdom = **[Nation of Ephraim *(descendants of Isaac)*] and [Nation of Judah *(descendants of Isaac)*]**} = [Descendent generation = *another generation grew up*] = [Golden Calves *(descendants of Isaac)*] = [Exiled to the land of (?)_(?)] = [End of the Ram Age *(Ending Timeline marker)*]

The next thing you must do is look closely at the bold portion in the following description of Zechariah 1:18-19 below,

[Then I looked up – **and there before me were four horns!** I asked the angel who was speaking to me, "What are these?" He answered me, **"These are the horns that scattered Judah, Israel and Jerusalem]**

Next, remove the following descriptions from the verses and look closely below,

[Judah, Israel and Jerusalem]

(Note26: Within this description reveals two major clues. For example: One of the nation's (Judah or Israel) corresponds to the kingdom of Jerusalem, and the other does not!)

Here is the next clue: The tribe of Benjamin corresponds to the nation of Judah and will emerge into the following kingdom: [The kingdom of Jerusalem].

(Note27: The nation of Judah will emerge into the kingdom of Jerusalem after the second exodus period in the time of the Persian Empire (after the fall of the Ram Age). Thus, during the rise of Babylon (before the second exodus), only the nation of Judah would find themselves exiled to Babylon.)

*(Note28: **Jacob** the second born son of Isaac will come to represent the father of the Kingdom of Jerusalem (the western hill country). This revelation reveals the meaning behind the description **'and to Isaac I gave Jacob and Esau. I assigned the hill country of Seir to Esau, but Jacob and his family went down to Egypt'** (land of the west) - Joshua 24:4)*

*(Note29: This description is also deceptive and reveals a trap. For example: Jacob does not represent the father of Egypt, nor does he and his family go to the land of Egypt. This description **'but Jacob and his family went down to Egypt'** is symbolic and refers to the land in the west that borders the land of Egypt. The land that borders Egypt represents the land of Jerusalem (western hill country land). Therefore, Jacob and his family went down towards the land of Egypt but settled in the land that would become known as the Kingdom of Jerusalem))*

(Note30: If you look closely at the description of Zechariah 1:18-19 (Judah, Israel and Jerusalem) you will discover the land of Israel corresponds to the Nation of Ephraim. Thus, the name of a kingdom corresponding to Ephraim is missing. The second clue is revealed in the description of 1ˢᵀ Kings)

Look closely at the bold portion in the description of 1ˢᵀ Kings 16:23-24 below,

> [In the thirty-first year of Asa king of Judah, Omri became king of Israel, and he reigned twelve years, six of them in Tirzah. **He bought the hill of Samaria from Shemer for two talents of silver and built a city on the hill, calling it Samaria, after Shemer**, the name of the former owner of the hill]

(Note31: The hill of Samaria is symbolic and represents the kingdom, known as the kingdom of Samaria. Thus, the nation of Ephraim will emerge into a kingdom of their own in the time of the Assyrian Empire (before the second exodus period))

Here is the next clue: The following ten tribes: 'Ephraim, Manasseh, Naphtali, Dan, Asher, Issachar, Zebulon, Simeon, Reuben, and Gad' corresponds to the nation of Ephraim *(land of Israel)* and will emerge into the following kingdom: [The kingdom of Samaria].

(Note32: This revelation reveals the meaning behind the following description 'The ten horns you saw are ten kings who have not yet received a kingdom – Revelation 17:12.' Thus, the nation of Ephraim, also known as the land of Israel, will finally emerge into a kingdom of their own, and will become the Kingdom of Samaria)

*(Note33: **Esau** the elder son of Isaac will come to represent the father of the Kingdom of Samaria. The Kingdom of Samaria (land of the eastern hill country) represents the land of Israel, also known as the eastern hill country, the land of Seir. This revelation reveals the meaning behind the verses of Genesis 36:8-9 – **'So Esau (that is, Edom) settled in the hill country of Seir. This is the account of the family line of Esau, the father of the Edomites in the hill country of Seir'**. Thus, Esau, the 'father of the Edomites' (the eastern hill country, the land of Seir), also represents the father of the Samaritans (the eastern hill country, the land of Israel))*

The next thing you must do is bring back the following revelation revealed by the short horn and merge the revelations together regarding the Kingdoms of Samaria and Jerusalem in their proper places as seen below,

- [Short horn] = {Nation of Isaac} = {Father of the first two nations born out of the 1ˢᵗ kingdom = {[Nation of Ephraim *(descendants of Isaac)* = **Kingdom of Samaria *(descendants of Esau)***] and [Nation of Judah *(descendants of Isaac)* = **Kingdom of Jerusalem *(descendants of Jacob)***]} = [Descendent generation = *another generation grew up*] = [Golden Calves *(descendants of Isaac)*] = [Exiled to the land of (?)_(?)] = [End of the Ram Age]

*(Note34: The four prominent horns (Zechariah 1:18-19), did not scatter the nations. Thus, it was the 4ᵗʰ prominent horn (as representing a 4ᵗʰ kingdom) that revealed how the nations of Ephraim and Judah scattered themselves when they broke apart from the City of David (4ᵗʰ Kingdom). This revelation corresponds to the following description '**Ephraim broke away from Judah**' - Isaiah 7:17)*

The next thing you must do is merge the revelations regarding the two kingdoms together with the base decoder regarding the 4ᵗʰ prominent horn in its proper places as seen below,

{4ᵀᴴ prominent horn} = [7ᵀᴴ head = 7ᵀᴴ hill = 7ᵀᴴ king] = [4ᵀᴴ beast (ten horns)] = [4ᵀᴴ kingdom = Divided Kingdom = City of David:

{Ten Horns} = [Ten kings = Ten tribes = *I will take the kingdom from his son's hands and give you ten tribes* = Tribes of: Ephraim, Manasseh, Naphtali, Dan, Asher, Issachar, Zebulon, Simeon, Reuben, and Gad = Jeroboam king of Ephraim = Nation of Ephraim (land of Israel) = *who are yet to receive a kingdom of their own* = **Kingdom of Samaria *(descendants of Esau)***]

{Beast} = [single tribe = *I will give one tribe to his son* = Tribe of Benjamin = *remained in the city* = Nation of Judah = Rehoboam king of Judah = **Kingdom of Jerusalem *(descendants of Jacob)***]

The next thing you must do is look carefully at the bold portions in the following description of Daniel 7:24.

> [**Ten kings will emerge from this kingdom**. After them, **another king would arise** different from the earlier ones, **he would subdue three kings**]

Next, remove the bold portions of this description in numbered order as seen below,

1- Ten kings will emerge from this kingdom
2- another king would arise
3- he would subdue three kings

*(Note35: Each of the three descriptions above reveal three more vital clues. The first step is to reveal the mystery of the following description '**Ten kings will emerge from this kingdom**.' The clue is hidden behind the revelation of the elements)*

Here is the next vital clue: The following ten kings *(ten horns)*, as representing ten tribes and revealed as the Nation of Ephraim *(land of Israel)* that emerges into the Kingdom of Samaria, will emerge from the following element associated with the City of David: [The Kingdom of Clay]!

(Note36: To solve the mystery of who the mystery king represents (another king would arise), you must first solve the mystery behind the three kings he will subdue. To start, you must look closely at the description of Daniel 7:20)

Next, look closely at the bold portion in the description of Daniel 7:20 below,

> [I also wanted to know about the ten horns on its head **and about the other horn that came up, before which three of them fell**]

*(Note37: The following **three subdued kings** (Daniel 7:24) correspond to **three fallen horns** (Daniel 7:20). To uncover the identity of the fallen horns (that are three subdued kings) you must use the base decoder to play a game called 'The Process of Elimination')*

The first thing you must do is bring back the following revelation revealed by the base decoder and look closely at the bolded portion,

- **{Two horns} = [two heads = two hills = two kings]**

    {Large horn} = [3RD head = 3RD hill = 3RD king]

    {1^{ST} prominent horn} = [4TH head = 4TH hill = 4TH king] = [1ST beast = lion = 1ST kingdom]

    {2^{ND} prominent horn} = [5TH head = 5TH hill = 5TH king] = [2ND beast = bear = 2ND kingdom]

    {3^{RD} prominent horn} = [6TH head = 6TH hill = 6TH king] = [3RD beast = leopard = 3RD kingdom]

    {4^{TH} prominent horn} = [7TH head = 7TH hill = 7TH king] = [4TH beast = ? = 4TH kingdom]

Next, subtract the **{Ram's two horns** *(representing two kings)***}** from the base decoder!

(Note38: The ram's two horns (representing two kings), already fell by the rising power of the goat's large horn (representing a third king) - Daniel 8:5-7). Thus, they do not correspond to any of the three fallen horns that are three subdued kings)

(Note39: This mystery king (who subdue three kings) does not subdue the ram's two horns but will subdue the goat's large horn (representing a third king), who was responsible for bringing the ram's two horns to ruin as revealed by the description of Daniel 8:7))

The second thing you must do is bring back the following revelation revealed by the base decoder and look closely at the next bolded portion as seen below,

- **{Large horn} = [3RD head = 3RD hill = 3RD king]**

    {1ST prominent horn} = [4TH head = 4TH hill = 4TH king] = [1ST beast = lion = 1ST kingdom]

    {2ND prominent horn} = [5TH head = 5TH hill = 5TH king] = [2ND beast = bear = 2ND kingdom]

    {3RD prominent horn} = [6TH head = 6TH hill = 6TH king] = [3RD beast = leopard = 3RD kingdom]

    {4TH prominent horn} = [7TH head = 7TH hill = 7TH king] = [4TH beast = ? = 4TH kingdom]

Next, subtract the **{Goat's large horn** *(representing a third king)***}** from the base decoder!

(Note40: The goat's large horn (3rd king) fell reaching the height of its power as revealed by Daniel 8:8))

(Note41: The goat's large horn (3rd king) represents one of three fallen horns, as representing, one of three subdued kings))

The third thing you must do is bring back the following revelation revealed by the base decoder and look closely at the next bolded portions as seen below,

- **{1ST prominent horn} = [4TH head = 4TH hill = 4TH king] = [1ST beast = lion = 1ST kingdom]**

- **{2ND prominent horn} = [5TH head = 5TH hill = 5TH king] = [2ND beast = bear = 2ND kingdom]**

{3RD prominent horn} = [6TH head = 6TH hill = 6TH king] = [3RD beast = leopard = 3RD kingdom]

{4TH prominent horn} = [7TH head = 7TH hill = 7TH king] = [4TH beast = ? = 4TH kingdom]

(Note42: There is a hidden clue found in the description of Daniel 2:38-39 that is needed to solve the mystery regarding the next fallen horns, as representing, the next subdued kings)

Look closely at the bold portion in the following description of Daniel 2:38-39 below,

[In your hands he has placed mankind and the beasts of the field and the birds of the air. Wherever they live, he has made you ruler over them all. **You are that head of gold. After you, another kingdom will rise, inferior to yours.** Next, a third kingdom, one of bronze, will rule over the whole earth]

(Note43: To identify the hidden clue, you must merge the bold descriptions of Daniel 2:38-39, with the following revelations revealed by the base decoder regarding the 1st and 2nd prominent horns)

The next clue is revealed by the illustration below,

- [1st prominent horn = 4th king] = [1st kingdom = *You are that head of gold*]

- [2nd prominent horn = 5th king] = [2nd kingdom = *After you, another kingdom will rise, inferior to yours*]

(Note44: The following description 'another kingdom will rise, inferior to yours' is symbolic and refers to the element that is considered inferior to the element of gold. This element represents the element of silver. This revelation will be revealed in more detail in the later chapters. These two prominent horns, the 4th

king (1st kingdom of Gold) and 5th king (2nd kingdom of silver), represent the final two fallen horns, as representing, the final two subdued kings. The fall of both kingdoms is depicted in the following description of Daniel - **Next, a third kingdom, one of bronze, will rule over the whole earth** – Daniel 2:39. Thus, the description 'will rule over the whole earth' represents the fall of the Kingdoms of Clay, Gold, and Silver))

Next, subtract the {**1st and 2nd prominent horns** *(representing a fourth and fifth king)*} from the base decoder!

(Note45: Out of the five kings (five horns) removed from the base decoder only three of them correspond to three fallen horns, as representing, three subdued kings))

Here is the [**2nd vital clue**]: The three fallen horns, representing three subdued kings is revealed by the following illustration below:

- {Large horn *(goat)*} = [3rd head = 3rd hill = 3rd king] = [**1st fallen horn = 1st subdued king**]

- {1st prominent horn} = [4th head = 4th hill = 4th king] = [**2nd fallen horn = 2nd subdued king**]

- {2nd prominent horn} = [5th head = 5th hill = 5th king] = [**3rd fallen horn = 3rd subdued king**]

To reveal the mystery king who subdues three kings *(representing three fallen horns)*, you must bring back the description of Daniel 2:39 and look closely at the bold description of the verse.

[After you, another kingdom will rise, inferior to yours. **Next, a third kingdom, one of bronze, will rule over the whole earth**]

(Note46: The 3rd kingdom of bronze subdues the kingdoms of clay, gold and silver. Thus, the element of bronze trumps the elements of clay, gold and silver. This revelation will also be revealed in more detail in the later chapters. This description **'will rule over the whole earth'** *represents the rise of a powerful king, in whose rising power, will subdue the other kings that came before it.)*

The next thing you must do is bring back the following two kings that remain in the base decoder!

- {3RD prominent horn} = [6TH head = 6TH hill = 6TH king] = [3RD beast = leopard = 3RD kingdom]

- {4TH prominent horn} = [7TH head = 7TH hill = 7TH king] = [4TH beast = ? = 4TH kingdom]

Next, look closely at the bold portion in the following description of Revelation 17:10 below,

[Five have fallen, **one is**, **the other has not yet come**; but when he does come, he must remain for a little while]

The final thing you must do is remove the bold portion from the verse and merge them with the two remaining kings into the correct places.

- {3RD prominent horn} = [6TH head = 6TH hill] = [6TH king = **One is**] = [3RD beast = leopard = 3RD kingdom of Bronze *(will rule over the whole earth)*]

- {4TH prominent horn} = [7TH head = 7TH hill] = [7TH king = **the other has not yet come**] = [4TH beast = ? = 4TH kingdom of Iron]

*(Note47: The **7th king** (the other, has not yet come) represents a **4th kingdom** and corresponds to the following description **'Finally, there will be a fourth kingdom, strong as iron'** – Daniel 2:40. The reason this description is written 'the other, has not yet come,' means this 7th king has not yet emerged to power! This description 'one is' reveals the emergence of a powerful king and will correspond to the description 'which will rule over all the earth'))*

The final thing you must do is bring back the following description.

2- another king would arise

Here is the **[3rd vital clue]:** The mystery king (who would arise) corresponds to the description **'one is'** and represents the following king who would arise to bring about the fall of three fallen horns as representing three subdued kings: [6th king *(as representing the 3rd kingdom, of bronze)*]!

*(Note48: This revelation reveals the meaning behind the description of Revelation 17:10: 'Five have fallen **(five horns as representing five kings)**, one is **(3rd prominent horn as representing a 6th king)**, the other, has not yet come **(4th prominent horn as representing a 7th king)**, but when he does come; he must remain for a little while!')*

Congratulations!!! You have successfully completed the [2nd test]!

The next thing you must do is solve the mystery concealed behind the **[3rd test]**.

[The beast who once was, and now is not, is an eighth king. He belongs to the seven and is going to his destruction]

(Note: To solve this mystery you must uncover the revelation revealed behind this mysterious king)

THE MYSTERIOUS 8TH KING

The first thing you must do is look carefully at the bold portion in the following description of Daniel 8:9.

> [**Out of one of them came another horn**, which started small but grew in power to the south and to the east and toward the Beautiful Land]

(Note2: Within one of the four prominent horns reveals a hidden clue to solving the mystery of this description)

To reveal the mystery, bring back the following revelations regarding the four prominent horns revealed by the base decoder and merge the bold descriptions together regarding this mysterious prominent horn.

$\{1^{ST}$ prominent horn$\}$ = [4TH head = 4TH hill = 4TH king] = [1ST beast = lion = 1ST kingdom]

$\{2^{ND}$ prominent horn$\}$ = [5TH head = 5TH hill = 5TH king] = [2ND beast = bear = 2ND kingdom]

$\{3^{RD}$ prominent horn$\}$ = [6TH head = 6TH hill = 6TH king] = [3RD beast = leopard = 3RD kingdom]

- $\{4^{TH}$ prominent horn *(Out of one of them came another horn)*$\}$ = [7TH head = 7TH hill = 7TH king] = [4TH beast = ? = 4TH kingdom]

(Note3: Within the 4th prominent horn reveals the mystery. For example: There is a little mysterious horn that emerges from within the 4th prominent horn and will itself emerge to power to become a prominent horn. This revelation corresponds to the following description **'started small but grew in power'** *– Daniel 8:9, as well as the following description of Revelation* **'He belongs to the seven'** *– Revelation 17:11. The reason as to why this little mysterious horn belongs to the seven is because it emerges from one of the seven horns. Thus, it will emerge from the 4th prominent horn)*

Here is the next clue: This mysterious horn represents the following revelation: [a 5th prominent horn]!

This revelation is revealed by the following illustration:

{5TH prominent horn}

- {4TH prominent horn *(Out of one of them came another horn)*} = [7TH head = 7TH hill = 7TH king] = [4TH beast = ? = 4TH kingdom]

The next thing you must do is look closely at the bold description of Daniel 7:8.

[While I was thinking about the horns, **there before me was another horn, a little one, which came up among them**; and three of the first horns were uprooted before it]

(Note4: This description is written deceptively and reveals another important clue. For example: The following description 'there before me was another horn, a little one, which came up among them' does not represent the mysterious king or horn that subdued three kings as representing three fallen horns. As revealed previously, that mysterious king represented a 6th king and corresponded to the bold portion of this description **'and about the other horn that came up**, *before which three of them fell' - Daniel 7:20.)*

To reveal the clue, bring back the following revelations regarding the four prominent horns and merge the bold descriptions together regarding this mysterious prominent horn.

{1ST prominent horn} = [4TH head = 4TH hill = 4TH king] = [1ST beast = lion = 1ST kingdom]

{2ND prominent horn} = [5TH head = 5TH hill = 5TH king] = [2ND beast = bear = 2ND kingdom]

{3RD prominent horn} = [6TH head = 6TH hill = 6TH king] = [3RD beast = leopard = 3RD kingdom]

- {4TH prominent horn *(Out of one of them came another horn)*} = [7TH head = 7TH hill = 7TH king] = [4TH beast = ? = Ten horns *(there before me was another horn, a little one, which came up among them)* = 4TH kingdom]

Here is the next clue: The mysterious little horn corresponds to a 5th prominent horn and represents the following king: [8th king]!

{Important Note...The mysterious little horn will emerge from two places. On one hand, it will emerge from the 4th prominent horn as corresponding to the description (Out of one of them came another horn) and will emerge into the 5th prominent horn. And on the other, it will emerge from the ten horns of the 4th beast as corresponding to the description (there before me was another horn, a little one, which came up among them) and will emerge into an 8th king. Thus, the 4th beast with ten horns as also representing a 7th king, will give rise to the 8th king. This revelation reveals the meaning behind the description - The beast, who once was and now is not, is an eighth king. He belongs to the seven (as representing the 7th king) – Revelation 17:11)}

This revelation is revealed by the following illustration:

{5TH prominent horn}　　　　　　　　　　　　　　　　　　{8TH King}

- {4TH prominent horn *(Out of one of them came another horn)*} = [7TH head = 7TH hill = 7TH **king**] = [4TH beast = ? = Ten horns *(there before me was another horn, a little one, which came up among them)* = 4TH kingdom]

The next thing you must do is merge the revelation revealed by the 5th prominent horn.

- {5TH **prominent horn**} = [8th king]

The next thing you must do is look carefully at the bold portion in the following description of Revelation 17:3.

[Then the angel carried me away in the Spirit into a desert. There I saw a woman sitting on a **scarlet beast that was covered with blasphemous names and had seven heads and ten horns**]

(Note5: There are two vital clues revealed within this description)

THE SCARLET BEAST

The first thing you must do is remove the following bold descriptions from the verses.

[Scarlet beast]   **[Seven heads]**   **[Ten horns]**

*(Note6: The first step to revealing the 1st clue is to begin by merging the following descriptions (**Scarlet beast**) and (**ten horns**) together as seen in the illustration below)*

[Scarlet beast] - [Ten horns] = ?

Here is the next clue: The (scarlet beast) and (ten horns) corresponds to the following beast: [4th beast (with ten horns)]!

Next, bring back the revelation regarding the 4th prominent horn revealed by the base decoder and merge the revelation together regarding the scarlet beast and ten horns into the correct place as seen below,

[4TH prominent horn} = [7TH head = 7TH hill = 7TH king] = [4TH beast = {beast *(Scarlet beast)* = ten horns *(ten horns)*]

Next, look closely at the final description as seen below,

[Seven heads] = ?

(Note7: The second step to revealing the 1st vital clue is to merge the next following description which is the (seven heads) with the description of Revelation 17:9, to reveal another hidden clue. For example: The objective is to figure out which of the seven heads correspond to the scarlet beast and ten horns (representing a 4th beast))

Here is the next clue: The seven heads correspond to the following revelation: [7th head that is a 7th hill on which the woman sits]!

Next, bring back the revelation regarding the 4th prominent horn revealed by the base decoder and merge the revelations into the correct places as seen below,

- [4ᵀᴴ prominent horn} = [**7ᵀᴴ head = 7ᵀᴴ hill**] = [7ᵀᴴ king] = [beast *(Scarlet beast)* = ten horns *(ten horns)*] = [4ᵀᴴ beast = ?]

Here is the [**1ˢᵗ vital clue**]: The scarlet beast and ten horns corresponds to the 4th beast (with ten horns) as well as a 7th head that is a 7th hill, on which the woman sits. Thus, representing the following king: [7th king]!

(Note8: This revelation will be brought back in the next chapter to reveal another great revelation. The next step is to uncover the revelation regarding the 2nd vital clue!)

THE WOMAN

The next thing you must do is look closely at the next bold portion in the same previous description of Revelation 17:3.

> [Then the angel carried me away in the Spirit into a desert. **There I saw a woman sitting** on a scarlet beast that was covered with blasphemous names and had seven heads and ten horns]

*(Note9: There are two steps you must take to reveal the second vital clue. The first step is to understand the paradox between the following two descriptions: '**Out of one of them came another horn**' – Daniel 8:9 and '**While I was thinking about the horns, there before me was another horn, a little one, which came up among them**'– Daniel 7:8))*

(Note10: Example1: If you look closely at the two descriptions of Daniel 8:9 and Daniel 7:8, you will discover the woman is not sitting as described; but is emerging from two places)

*(Note11: Example2: The woman corresponds to an emerging 5th prominent horn that is emerging from the 4th prominent horn as revealed in the description '**Out of one of them came another horn**' – Daniel 8:9. And she represents an emerging 8th king that emerges from the 4th beast's ten horns (representing a 7th king) as revealed in the description '**While I was thinking about the horns, there before me was another horn, a little one, which came up among them**'– Daniel 7:8))*

Here is the [**2nd vital clue**]: The **woman** *(sitting on the scarlet beast)* corresponds to an emerging **5th prominent horn** that emerges from the 4th prominent horn *(Out of one of them came another horn)* as well as an **emerging 8th king** that emerges from the 4th beast's ten horns as representing a 7th king *(there before me was another horn, a little one, which came up among them)*, and she represents the following emerging beast that emerges from the 4th beast *(corresponding to the scarlet beast)* : [an emerging **5th beast**]!

This revelation is revealed by the following illustration:

$$\{5^{TH} \text{ prominent horn} = \mathbf{5^{th} \text{ beast}} = 8^{TH} \text{ King}\}$$

- $\{4^{TH}$ prominent horn *(Out of one of them came another horn)*$\} = [7^{TH}$ head $= 7^{TH}$ hill $= 7^{TH}$ king$] = [4^{TH}$ beast $= ? =$ Ten horns *(there before me was another horn, a little one, which came up among them)* $= 4^{TH}$ kingdom$]$

Next, bring back the following revelations regarding the 5th prominent horn and merge the revelations together regarding the woman in the correct places as seen below,

- $\{5^{th}$ prominent horn$\} = \mathbf{[5^{th} \text{ beast} = Woman]} = [8^{th}$ king$]$

(Note 12: This revelation reveals the meaning behind the description of Revelation 17:11- 'The beast (5ᵗʰ beast) who once was (5ᵗʰ prominent horn), and now is not, is an eighth king. He belongs to the seven (4ᵗʰ prominent horn = 4ᵗʰ beast = 7ᵗʰ king) and is going to his destruction')

{Important note... There is a second part to this revelation that will be revealed in detail within the 2nd Chapter that will expose a great deception regarding the gender in this description '**He belongs to the seven and is going to his destruction.** This revelation will be revealed behind the understanding of this description '**and among the lampstand was someone like a son of man'**– *Revelation 1:12*}

Congratulations! You have successfully completed the [3rd test]!

The next thing you must do is solve the mystery concealed behind the **[4ᵗʰ test]**.

[This calls for a mind with wisdom. If anyone has insight, **let him calculate the number of the beast, for it is man's number**. His number is 666]

(Note: The bold portion of this description reveals three vital clues that are needed to uncover the mystery)

The first thing you must do is disassemble the bold description and place them into an equation.

- let him calculate the number of the beast = ?
- for it is man's number = ?

To start you must reveal the [1st vital clue] hidden behind the following equation:

- (let him calculate the number of the beast) = **[?]**

CALCULATE THE NUMBER OF THE BEAST

The first thing you must do is look closely at the bold portion in the following description of Revelation 16:13-14 below,

> [**Then I saw three evil spirits that looked like frogs; they came out of the mouth of the dragon, out of the mouth of the beast and out of the mouth of the false prophet**. They are spirits of demons performing miraculous signs, and they go out to the kings of the whole world, to gather them for the battle on the great day of God Almighty]

Next, remove the bold portion of the description below,

> [Then I saw three evil spirits that looked like frogs; they came out of the mouth of the dragon, out of the mouth of the beast and out of the mouth of the false prophet]

(Note2: If you look closely at this description, you will discover there are three evil spirits that looked like frogs in the description. To understand the mystery of this, you must reveal the true image of the three spirits (that looked like frogs). The objective in this equation is to reveal the mystery beast (three times) in the order that they will appear. As will soon be revealed, one of the true image's referring to one of the spirit's that looked like a frog has already been previously identified))

THE SCARLET BEAST

The first thing you must do is solve the mystery behind the description of Revelation 17:3.

[Then the angel carried me away in the Spirit into a desert. There I saw a woman sitting on a **scarlet beast** that was covered with blasphemous names and had **seven heads** and **ten horns**]

The next thing you must do as previously revealed is remove the bold portion from the verses.

[Scarlet beast]   [Seven heads]   [Ten horns]

(Note3: The first step as previously revealed is to begin by merging together the following two descriptions (Scarlet beast) and (ten horns) together as seen in the illustration below)

[Scarlet beast] – [Ten horns] = ?

Here is the next clue: The (scarlet beast) and (ten horns) corresponds to the following beast: [4th beast (with ten horns)]!

Next, bring back the revelation regarding the 4th prominent horn revealed by the base decoder and merge the revelation together regarding the scarlet beast and ten horns into the correct places as seen below,

[4TH prominent horn} = [7TH head = 7TH hill = 7TH king] = [4TH beast = {beast *(Scarlet beast)* = ten horns *(ten horns)*]

Next, look closely at the final description as seen below,

[Seven heads] = ?

*(Note4: The second step to revealing the 1st vital clue is to merge the next following description which is the (**seven heads**) with the description of Revelation 17:9 to reveal another hidden clue. For example: The objective is to figure out which of the seven heads correspond to the scarlet beast and ten horns (representing a 4th beast))*

Here is the next clue: The seven heads correspond to the following revelation: [7th head that is a 7th hill on which the woman sits]!

Next, bring back the revelation regarding the 4th prominent horn revealed by the base decoder and merge the revelations into the correct places as seen below,

[4TH prominent horn} = [7TH **head = 7TH hill**] = [7TH king] = [beast *(Scarlet beast)* = ten horns *(ten horns)*] = [4TH beast =?]

Here is the [final revelation]: The **scarlet beast** *(with ten horns)* corresponds to a **4th beast** *(with ten horns)* as well as a **7th head that is a 7th hill,** on which the woman sits. Thus, representing the following revelation: [The scarlet beast represents a 7th **king**]!

THE BEAST COMING OUT OF THE SEA

The second thing you must do is solve the mystery behind the description of Revelation 13:1.

[And the dragon stood on the shore of the sea. And I saw a **beast coming out of the sea. He had ten horns and seven heads, with ten crowns on his horns**, and on each head a blasphemous name]

The next thing you must do is remove the bold portion from the verses.

[Beast coming out of the sea]   [Ten horns]   [Seven heads]   [Ten crowns]

Next, look closely at the three descriptions as seen below,

[Beast coming out of the sea] - [Ten horns] – [Ten crowns] = ?

*(Note5: The ten crowns correspond to ten kings as representing ten horns. The next step is to merge the following three descriptions (**Beast coming out of the sea**), (**ten horns**) and (**ten crowns**) to reveal a hidden clue))*

Here is the next clue: The (Beast coming out of the sea), and (ten horns), and (ten crowns) corresponds to the following beast: [4th beast with ten horns *(representing ten crowns)*]!

Next, bring back the revelation regarding the 4th prominent horn revealed by the base decoder and merge the revelation together regarding the Beast coming out of the sea, the ten horns and ten crowns into the correct places.

[4TH prominent horn} = [7TH head = 7TH hill] = [7TH king] = [beast *(Beast coming out of the sea)* = ten horns *(ten horns and ten crowns)*] = [4TH beast =?]

Next, look closely at the final description as seen below,

[Seven heads] = ?

*(Note6: The next step is to merge the following description (**seven heads**), with the description of Revelation 17:9 to reveal another hidden clue. The objective is to figure out which of the seven heads correspond to the Beast coming out of the sea and ten horns and ten crowns (representing a 4th beast))*

Here is the next clue: The seven heads correspond to the following revelation: [7th head that is a 7th hill on which the woman sits]!

Next, bring back the revelation regarding the 4th prominent horn revealed by the base decoder and merge the revelations into the correct places.

- [4TH prominent horn} = [7TH **head** = 7TH **hill**] = [7TH king] = [beast *(Beast coming out of the sea)* = ten horns *(ten horns)* and *(ten crowns)*] = [4TH beast = ?]

Here is the [final revelation]: The **Beast coming out of the sea** *(with ten horns and ten crowns)* correspond to a **4**th **beast** with ten horns *(representing ten kings)* as well as a **7**th **head that is a 7**th **hill**, on which the woman sits. Thus, representing the following revelation: [The beast coming out of the sea represents a **7**th **king**]!

THE RED DRAGON

The third thing you must do is solve the mystery behind the description of Revelation 12:3.

[Then another sign appeared in heaven: an enormous **red dragon with seven heads and ten horns and seven crowns on his heads**]

The next thing you must do is remove the following description from the verses.

[Red dragon]   [Seven heads]   [Ten horns]   [Seven crowns]

Next, look closely at the two descriptions as seen below,

[Red dragon] - [Ten horns] = ?

*(Note7: The next step is to merge the following two descriptions (**Red dragon**) and (**ten horns**), to reveal another hidden clue)*

Here is the next clue: The (Red dragon) and (ten horns) correspond to the following beast: [4th beast (with ten horns)]!

Next, bring back the revelation regarding the 4th prominent horn revealed by the base decoder and merge the revelation together regarding the Red dragon and ten horns into the correct places.

- [4TH prominent horn} = [7TH head = 7TH hill = 7TH king] = [beast (***Red dragon***) = ten horns *(ten horns)*] = [4TH beast =?]

Next, look closely at the final two descriptions as seen below,

[Seven heads] - [Seven crowns] = ?

*(Note8: The seven heads correspond to seven crowns as representing seven kings. The next step is to merge the following two descriptions **(seven heads)** and **(seven crowns)**, with the description of Revelation 17:9, to reveal another hidden clue. The objective is to figure out which of the seven heads (that are seven crowns), correspond to the Red dragon and ten horns (representing a 4th beast))*

Here is the next clue: The seven heads and seven crowns correspond to the following: [7th head that is a 7th hill, on which the woman sits]!

Next, bring back the revelation regarding the 4th prominent horn revealed by the base decoder and merge the revelations into the correct places.

- [4TH prominent horn} = [7TH **head** = 7TH **crown** = 7TH **hill**] = [7TH king] = [beast *(Red dragon)* = ten horns] = [4TH beast =?]

Here is the [final revelation]: The **Red dragon** *(with ten horns)* corresponds to a **4th beast** *(with ten horns)* as well as a **7th head that is a 7th hill**, on which the woman sits. Thus, representing the following revelation: [The Red dragon represents a 7th king]!

The next thing you must do is display the revelations in the correct places to reveal the order of the beast that reflect each of the three evil spirits that looked like frogs as seen in the illustration below,

- [1st evil spirit *(look like a frog)* = **scarlet beast**] = [7th king]
- [2nd evil spirit *(look like a frog)* = **beast coming out of the sea**] = [7th king]
- [3rd evil spirit *(look like a frog)* = **red dragon**] = [7th king]

The next thing you must do is look carefully at the bold portion in the following description of Revelation 12:9.

[The great dragon was hurled down-that **ancient serpent** called the **devil**, or **Satan**, who leads the whole world astray]

Next, remove the bold portion of the descriptions from the verses as seen below,

- [**ancient serpent**]
- [**devil**]
- [**Satan**]

Next, bring back the following revelations previously revealed and merge the bold descriptions removed from the description of Revelation 12:9 into the correct places as seen below,

[1st evil spirit *(look like a frog)*] = [scarlet beast = **devil**] = [7th king]

[2nd evil spirit *(look like a frog)*] = [beast coming out of the sea = **ancient serpent**] = [7th king]

[3rd evil spirit *(look like a frog)*] = [red dragon = **Satan**] = [7th king]

Next, bring back the revelations revealed by the 4th prominent horn and merge the revelations revealed by the three evil spirits (which looks like frogs) with the 4th beast into the correct places as seen below,

[4TH prominent horn] = [7TH head = 7TH hill = 7TH king] = [4TH beast with ten horns = (**{scarlet beast = devil} = {beast coming out of the sea = ancient serpent} = {red dragon** *(iron teeth and bronze claws)* **= Satan** *(name of a man)***])}**

Here is the 1st vital clue: The following equation _ **let him calculate the number of the beast**_ represents the following beast: [4th beast]

FOR IT IS MAN NUMBER

The next step is to reveal the 2nd vital clue by unlocking the mystery behind the following description [**for it is man's number**]

The first thing you must do is look carefully at the bold portion in the description of Daniel Chapter 12:7 below,

> [The man clothed in linen, who was above the waters of the river, lifted his right hand and his left hand toward heaven, and I heard him swear by him who lives forever, saying, "**It will be for a time, times and half a time**. When the power of the holy people has been finally broken, all these things will be completed]

Next, remove the bold description from the verses as seen below,

- [It will be for a time, times and half a time]

(Note9: To reveal the mystery of this description you must first locate the translator hidden within the description of Daniel)

Look closely at the bold portion in the description of Daniel 9:25 below,

> [Know and understand this: From the issuing of the decree to restore and rebuild Jerusalem until the Anointed One, the ruler, comes, **there will be seven 'seven,' and sixty-two 'sevens'**]

Next, remove the bold description from the verse as seen below,

- [there will be seven 'seven,' and sixty-two 'sevens']

*(Note10: This description will enable you to translate: (a time, times and half a time) into [**seven 'seven,' and sixty-two 'sevens'**]! The mystery of the revelation will be revealed very shortly!)*

The next thing you must do is reveal the [Multiplier]!

To reveal the multiplier, look carefully at the bold portion in the following two descriptions below,

- Genesis 4:24 - [If Cain is avenged **seven times, then** Lamech seventy- **seven times**]

- Matthew 18:22 - [Jesus answered, "I tell you, not seven times, **but** seventy-**seven times**]

(Note11: The following description 'I tell you, not seven times' is written deceptively and contains a hidden clue. For example: This part of the description (~~"I tell you, not seven times~~) *is instructing us not to include this 'seven times' to solve the equation.)*

Next, remove only the bold portion from the two descriptions above and merge them together *(do not bold the following words 'then' and 'but').*

- Genesis 4:24 - [**(seven times)**, then – **(seven times)**]

- Matthew 18:22 - [but – **(seven times)**]

Next, merge the two bold descriptions with the un-bolded portion to reveal a mathematical equation,

- [**seven times** (*then*) **seven times** (*but*) **seven times**] = **(?)**

*(Note12: The word **(times)** is a representation for the symbol of multiplication **[x]** (Thus revealing the first Multiplier))*

Next, bring back the following two descriptions previously removed from the verses but look more closely at the bold portions of the descriptions that are not crossed out.

- [~~time, times~~ and half a **time**]

- [~~seven 'seven,'~~ **and sixty-two 'sevens**]

67

(Note13: The following two descriptions 'time, times' and 'seven 'seven' is also written deceptively and reveals another hidden clue. For example: These two descriptions ~~'time, times'~~ and ~~'seven 'seven'~~ are decoys and must be cancelled out)

Next, remove the un-bolded description 'and half a' from the first description.

Now, re-list the same two descriptions once more but look closely at the bold portion as seen below,

- [**time**]

- [and sixty-two '**sevens**]

(Note14: The word (***time***) in this description is also a representation for the symbol of multiplication [x] (Thus revealing the second Multiplier)))

Next, merge the second multiplier *(time)* with the un-bolded portion to reveal another mathematical equation *(do not bold the following words 'and sixty-two 'sevens')*,

- [and sixty-two *(**time**)* sevens] = **(?)**

Next, bring back both descriptions and merge them together to reveal two numeric equations as seen below,

- [**seven times** *(then)* **seven times** = ____? *(but)* **seven times**] = ____?
- [and sixty-two *(**time**)* sevens] = ____?

(Note15: In a numeric equation, the math would appear as the following: (7x7= (?) x 7= (?) and 62x7 = (?))

Next, use the Multiplier to mathematically calculate their sums as seen below,

- [Seven *(**time**)* seven = <u>**49**</u> *(**times**)* seven = <u>**343**</u>]
- [sixty-two *(**times**)* sevens = <u>**434**</u>]

(Note16: In a numeric equation, the math will appear as the following: 7x7=49x7=343. And 62x7=434)

68

Next, use Addition to calculate the total sum of both equations into a whole number as seen below,

- [343 + 434] = **777**

Here is the 2nd vital clue: The following equation _ **for it is man number**_ represents the following revelation: [777]

The next thing you must do is look closely at the next bold portion in the description of Daniel 7:19.

[Then **I wanted to know the true meaning of the fourth beast, which was different from all the others and most terrifying**, with its iron teeth and bronze claws-the beast that crushed and devoured its victims and trampled underfoot whatever was left]

Next, remove the following bold portion of the description from the verse. See below,

[I wanted to know the true meaning of the fourth beast, which was different from all the others and most terrifying]

*(Note17: The 4th beast that Daniel sees (**with its iron teeth and bronze claws-the beast that crushed and devoured its victims and trampled underfoot whatever was left**) does not represent a dragon! Many scholars have been deceived by the assumption. The 4th beast Daniel sees is revealed behind the crown he bears!)*

To reveal the identity of the 4th beast, bring back the previous revelation revealed by the 4th prominent horn as seen below,

[4TH prominent horn] = [7TH head = 7TH hill = 7TH king] = [4TH beast with ten horns = (**{scarlet beast = devil} = {beast coming out of the sea = ancient serpent} = {red dragon** *(iron teeth and bronze claws)* **= Satan** *(name of a man)***])}**

Here is the revelation. The **4th beast** corresponds to the following: [scarlet beast = devil] and [beast coming out of the sea = ancient serpent] and the [red dragon] and represents the name of the following man revealed by the symbolic number for man **777:** [Satan the 7th king].

*(Note18: The **4th beast** corresponds to the symbolic number for man **777**, which reveals the name of a man as representing the **7th king**. Thus, this part of the description 'with its iron teeth and bronze claws-the beast that crushed and devoured its victims and trampled underfoot whatever was left' corresponds to the following [scarlet beast = devil] and [beast coming out of the sea = ancient serpent] as representing the [red dragon]. However, the identity of the 4th beast is revealed behind the symbolic number for man **777**. This description **'who has not yet come'** reveals the revelation of how the 4th prominent horn as*

representing the 7th king as the 4th kingdom of Iron, has now emerged to challenge the 6th king (who represents the description 'one is'))

The next thing you must do is bring back the following revelations revealed previously regarding the two remaining kings left in the game called 'The Process of Elimination' as seen below,

- {3^(RD) **prominent horn**} = [6^(TH) **head** = 6^(TH) **hill** = 6^(TH) **king**] = [3^(RD) **beast** = 3^(RD) **kingdom**] = [**One is**]

- {4^(TH) **prominent horn**} = [7^(TH) **head** = 7^(TH) **hill** = 7^(TH) **king**] = [4^(TH) **beast** = 4^(TH) **kingdom**] = [the other has not yet come]

Next, subtract the {**Goat's 3rd prominent horn** *(as representing a 6th king)*} from the base decoder!

(Note19: This 6th king (as representing the description 'one is') has now fallen by the rise of the 7th king as representing the 4th beast (who represents the description 'the other has not yet come')! This revelation corresponds to the following description **'crushed and devoured its victims and trampled underfoot whatever was left'** *– Daniel 7:19)*

The final thing you must do is look carefully at the following description of Daniel 2:40 below,

[Finally, there will be a fourth kingdom, strong as iron – for iron breaks and smashes everything – and as iron breaks things to pieces, so it will crush and break all the others]

(Note20: The 3rd kingdom of bronze (who would rule over the earth), has now fallen by the rise of the 4th kingdom of Iron (Thus, the element of Iron trumps the elements of clay, gold, silver and bronze). These material elements are also symbolic and will be revealed in more detail in the later chapters)

Here is the [final revelation]: The **4th beast** corresponds to the symbolic number **777** and reveals the name of a man as representing **Satan the 7th king**, who corresponds to the description **'the other has not yet come,'** has now risen to power and will come to represent the most powerful king of the seven!

The next thing you must do is look closely at the bold portion in the description of Revelation 13:18.

[This calls for a mind with wisdom. If anyone has insight, let him calculate the number of the beast, for it is man's number. **His number is 666**]

*(Note21: Contrary to popular belief, this mystery number **666** does not represent the Anti-Christ, Satan or Nero Caesar, as some Scholars would have you believe! As revealed previously, the name Satan represents the 7th king only! And as also previously revealed, his number is 777, not 666, as you will soon uncover)*

HIS NUMBER IS 666

The first thing you must do is remove the description of Revelation 13:18 *(from its current place in the Bible)* and re-align it beneath the verse in the description of Revelation 17:11. See below,

> [{**Revelation 17:9**} - 'This calls for a mind with wisdom. The seven heads are seven hills on which the woman sits. (10) They are also seven kings. Five have fallen, one is, the other has not yet come; but when he does come, he must remain for a little while. (11) The beast, who once was and now is not, is an eighth king. He belongs to the seven and is going to his destruction. {**Revelation 13:18**} - This calls for wisdom. If anyone has insight, let him calculate the number of the beast, for it is man's number. His number is 666]

(Note22: These two descriptions above reveal a complete riddle. Within this riddle conceals a vital clue that reveals a great revelation. For example: There is a great deception that is visible in plain sight!)

To reveal the great deception, look closely at the bold descriptions from these two verses.

> [{Revelation 17:9} - 'This calls for a mind with wisdom. The seven heads are seven hills on which the woman sits. (10) They are also seven kings. Five have fallen, one is, the other has not yet come; but when he does come, he must remain for a little while. (11) **The beast, who once was and now is not, is an eighth king. He belongs to the seven and is going to his destruction**. {Revelation 13:18} - This calls for wisdom. If anyone has insight, let him calculate the number of the beast, for it is man's number. **His number is 666**]

Next, remove the two bold descriptions from the two verses and merge them together as seen below,

- **The beast, who once was and now is not, is an eighth king. He belongs to the seven and is going to his destruction. His number is 666**

Here is the next **[vital clue]**: This description **His number is 666** corresponds to the description **'The beast, who once was and now is not, is an eighth king'** and represents the symbolic number that reveals the following gender of man: [Woman the 8th king]!

*(Note23: The following description 'The beast, who once was and now is not' corresponds to the 5th beast as representing the woman as the 8th king. The word **'His'** in the description (**His** number is 666) is also symbolic and corresponds to the description **'and among the lampstands was someone like a son of man'** – Revelation 1:12. This revelation will be revealed in more detail in the 2nd chapter)*

Next, merge both revelations regarding the symbolic numbers for [man] and [woman] in the correct place as seen below,

- [Symbolic number for Man] = [four it is man's number = 777] = [Satan the 7th king]

- [Symbolic number for Woman] = [someone like a son of man = 666] = [? = 8th king]

(Note24: A prominent king has now emerged to challenge the most powerful king of the seven who remains in the game. The name of this prominent king will be revealed in the later chapters. There now stands two kings remaining in the game called 'The Process of Elimination!')

The final thing you must do is bring back the revelations regarding the 4th and 5th prominent horns and merge the revelations regarding their symbolic numbers 666 and 777 as seen below,

- **[777]** = [4TH prominent horn] = [7TH head = 7TH hill = 7TH king *(number of his name)*] = [4TH beast = {beast coming out of the sea = ancient serpent *(Leviathan the serpent beast)*} = {scarlet beast = devil} = {red dragon *(iron teeth and bronze claws)*}] = {Satan *(name of a man)*} = [4th kingdom]

- **[666]** = [5th prominent horn] = [8th king] = [5th beast = Woman]

*(Note25: This revelation reveals the meaning behind the description of Revelation 13:18- 'If anyone has insight, let him calculate the number of the beast, **(4th beast = Satan = 7TH King)** for it is man number **(777)**. His **(5th beast = someone like a son of man = 8th King)** number is 666))*

Congratulations!!! You have successfully completed the [4th test]!

CHAPTER TWO - 1st PHASE OF THE CRYPTEX PUZZLE- REVELATION OF THE SIGN

In this chapter, you must venture deeper into the realm of understanding between the two remaining kings. Their revelations will begin to lay the foundation for what will become the battleground that ignites the Great War between them. And it will all unfold at the threshing floor of the altar!

*(Note: The Great War between the two kings represents a war that takes place within the heavenly realms! This revelation will reveal the true meaning behind the bold portion in the description of Ephesians 6:12 – 'For our struggle is not against flesh and blood, but against the rulers, against the authorities, against the powers of this dark world **and against the spiritual forces of evil in the heavenly realms**!')*

The first thing you must do is look carefully at the bold portion in the following description of Revelation 1:12.

[I turned around to see the voice that was speaking to me. **And when I turned I saw seven golden lampstands**]

*(Note2: This description reveals a vital clue. For example: If you examine the verse of Revelation 1:20 - **'The seven stars are the angels of the seven churches, and the seven lampstands are the seven churches'**, you will discover it too is structurally written deceptively. The clue is revealed by merging the seven golden lampstands with the description of Revelation 17:9. For example: the seven golden lampstands correspond to seven heads that are seven hills, on which the woman sits.)*

Here is the [vital clue]: The **seven golden lampstands** correspond to **seven heads that are seven hills**, on which the woman sits and represents the following revelation: [The seven golden lampstands represent **Seven kings**]!

The next thing you must do is bring back the revelation revealed by the base decoder and merge the revelations together into the correct places as seen below,

{Two horns *(ram)*} = [two heads = two hills = two kings] = **[two golden lampstands]**

{Larger horn *(goat)*} = [third head = third hill = 3RD king] = **[3rd golden lampstand]**

{1^{ST} prominent horn} = [4TH head = 4TH hill = 4TH king] = **[4th golden lampstand]**

{2^{ND} prominent horn} = [5TH head = 5TH hill = 5TH king] = **[5th golden lampstand]**

{3^{RD} prominent horn} = [6TH head = 6TH hill = 6TH king] = **[6th golden lampstand]**

{4^{TH} prominent horn} = [7TH head = 7TH hill = 7TH king] = **[7th golden lampstand]**

The next thing you must do is look carefully at the bold portion in the following description of Zechariah 4:2.

> [Then the angel who talked with me returned and wakened me, as a man is wakened from his sleep. He asked me, "What do you see?" I answered, **"I see a solid gold lampstand with a bowl at the top and seven lights on it, with seven channels to the lights**]

(Note3: This description also reveals another vital clue. For example: The solid gold lampstand in this description is different from the seven golden lampstands outlined in the description of Revelation 1:12. To reveal this hidden clue, merge the solid gold lampstand with the description of Revelation 17:11)

Here is the [2nd vital clue]: The **solid gold lampstand** corresponds to the following description **'The beast who once was, and now is not'** and represents the following revelation: [**Solid gold lampstand** represents an **8th King**]!

The next thing you must do is bring back the base decoder regarding the 5th prominent horn and merge the revelations together into the correct place as seen below,

$\{$5th prominent horn$\}$ = [5th beast = Woman] = [8th king = **Solid gold lampstand**]

The next thing you must do is look carefully at the bold portion in the following description of Revelation 1:12.

> [**and among the lampstands was someone like a son of man,** dressed in a robe reaching down to his feet and with a golden sash around his chest]

*(Note4: This description reveals another vital clue which reveals a great revelation. For example: There is a paradox between the following two descriptions of Revelation 1:12 and Zechariah 4:2. This description **'Someone like a son of man'** that is standing among the seven golden lampstands corresponds to the **solid gold lampstand** - Zechariah 4:2. This solid gold lampstand also corresponds to this description **'the beast who once was and now is not, is an eighth king'**)*

To understand this, bring back the following revelation revealed by the complete riddle. Look closely at the bold descriptions from the two verses.

> [{Revelation 17:9} - 'This calls for a mind with wisdom. The seven heads are seven hills on which the woman sits. (10) They are also seven kings. Five have fallen, one is, the other has not yet come; but when he does come, he must remain for a little while. (11) **The beast, who once was and now is not, is an eighth king.** He belongs to the seven and is going to his destruction. {Revelation 13:18} - This calls for wisdom. If anyone has insight, let him calculate the number of the beast, for it is man's number. **His number is 666**]

Next, merge the two bold descriptions revealed in the riddle with the following two descriptions **'solid gold lampstand'** and **'someone like a son of man'**. Look closely at the following illustration below,

- The beast, who once was and now is not, is an eighth king = Someone like a son of man = solid gold lampstand = His number is 666

Here is the [3rd vital clue]: The descriptions **(Someone like a son of man)** correspond to the **(solid gold lampstand)** and represents the following gender that reveals the symbolic number for woman (666): [woman the 8th king]!

{**Important note…** The following description **'Someone like a son of man'** is symbolic and does not represent a man. This description refers to the gender of woman who derives from man. This revelation corresponds to the bold part of this description 'The man said, "This is now bone of my bones and flesh of my flesh; **she shall be called 'woman,' for she was taken out of man.'** - Genesis 2:23. This part of the description 'for she was taken out of man' reveals the meaning behind this description **'He** (someone like a son of man) **belongs to the seven**}

The next thing you must do is bring back the base decoder regarding the 5th prominent horn and merge the revelations together into the correct places as seen below,

{5th prominent horn} = [5th beast = Woman = **Someone like a son of man** = 8th king] = [Solid gold lampstand]

(Note5: If the solid gold lampstand (8th king) represents a woman (someone like a son of man), why then is she standing among the seven golden lampstands (representing seven kings)? To solve this mystery, you must first follow the seven golden lampstands (also representing seven angels) to the direction of the upper gate, which faces north. Because, they have been summoned to appear before the altar)

The seven golden lampstands

Look closely at the bold portion in the following description of Ezekiel 9:1 below,

[Then I heard him call out in a loud voice, "Bring the guards of the city here, each with a weapon in his hand." **And I saw six men coming from the direction of the upper gate, which faces north, each with a deadly weapon in his hand.** With them was a man clothed in linen who had a writing kit at his side. They came in and stood beside the bronze altar]

(Note6: Within this description reveals a hidden clue. To reveal the clue, you must merge the following description 'I saw six men' with the description of Revelation 17:9. For example: The six men correspond to six heads that are six hills, on which the woman sits.)

Here is the next clue: The **six men** *(six golden lampstands)* coming from the direction of the upper gate corresponds to **'six heads that are six hills**, on which the woman sits' and represents the following revelation: [The six men represent **six kings**].

(Note7: Within the description of Ezekiel 9:1 reveals another hidden clue. For example: There is a 7th man (also representing a 7th king) that is missing from this very description 'coming from the direction of the upper gate which faces north.' Also, the 7th man does not correspond to this description 'With them was a man clothed in linen who had a writing kit at his side' - Ezekiel 9:2))

To solve this mystery, you must look closely at the two bold descriptions below,

- Job 1:6 - [One day the angels came to present themselves before the Lord, **and Satan also came with them**]

- Job 2:1 - [On another day the angels came to present themselves before the Lord, **and Satan also came with them to present himself before him**]

Here is the next clue: **Satan** corresponds to a **'seventh head that is a seventh hill**, on which the woman sits' and represents the following man: [the 7th man].

*(Note8: These **six men** (six golden lampstands), including **Satan the 7th man** (7th golden lampstand) who were summoned to appear before the altar reveals another paradox. For example: The following description **'They came in and stood beside the bronze altar'** (as representing seven men) corresponds to the following description **'And when I turned I saw seven golden lampstands'** - Revelation 1:12 (standing before the throne)*

The next thing you must do is bring back the revelation regarding the base decoder and merge the revelations together into the correct places as seen below,

{Two horns (*ram*)} = [two heads = two hills = two kings] = [two golden lampstands = **1st and 2nd men**]

{Larger horn (*goat*)} = [third head = third hill = 3RD king] = [3rd golden lampstand = **3rd man**]

{1ST prominent horn} = [4TH head = 4TH hill = 4TH king] = [4th golden lampstand = **4th man**]

{2ND prominent horn} = [5TH head = 5TH hill = 5TH king] = [5th golden lampstand = **5th man**]

{3RD prominent horn} = [6TH head = 6TH hill = 6TH king] = [6th golden lampstand = **6th man**]

{4TH prominent horn} = [7TH head = 7TH hill = 7TH king] = [7th golden lampstand = **7th man**] = **[Satan]**

(Note9: If seven men were summoned before the threshing floor of the altar. Who then, is standing in their mist? Within the description of Ezekiel 9:2 reveals the hidden clue!)

Look closely at the bold description in verses of Ezekiel 9:2 below,

> **[With them was a man clothed in linen who had a writing kit at his side.** They came in and stood beside the bronze altar]

*(Note10: This description reveals another paradox. For example: The **man clothed in linen** is symbolic and corresponds to the description 'Someone like a son of man (dressed in a robe reaching down to his feet).' Thus, representing the **solid gold lampstand**. To reveal the clue, you must merge the man clothed in linen with the description of Revelation 17:11)*

Here is the next clue: The **man clothed in linen** corresponds to the description '**someone like a son of man, dressed in a robe**' as well as the description '**the beast who once was and now is not**' and represents the gender of the following king: [woman the 8th king].

(Note11: This revelation reveals the meaning behind the following description 'I see a solid gold lampstand' – Zechariah 4:1))

The next thing you must do is bring back the base decoder regarding the 5th prominent horn and merge the revelation into the correct place as seen below,

> [5th prominent horn] = [Solid gold lampstand = Someone like a son of man = **Man clothed in linen (writing kit at his side)** = 8th king] = [5th beast = Woman]

(Note12: The next step is to go before the throne and stand before the eight golden lampstands. There is a very important revelation soon to be revealed and it begins by unlocking the mystery behind the description of Mark 10:40)

The next thing you must do is look closely at the description of Mark 10:40.

> [but to sit at my right or left is not for me to grant. These places belong to those for whom they have been prepared]

(Note13: There is an important vital clue revealed by this description. This clue is revealed by uncovering the revelation into whom the right and left places have been prepared for.)

The left place is prepared for the following king

To uncover the mystery of whom the left place has been prepared for, you must look closely at the following description of Revelation 7:2.

[Then I saw another angel coming up from the east, having the seal of the living God]

(Note14: The angel (coming up from the east) reveals a major clue. For example: The mighty angel is symbolic and corresponds to a certain golden lampstand who was summoned to appear before the altar (coming from the direction of the upper gate, which faces north). Thus, the direction 'which faces north' corresponds to the description 'coming up from the east' (thus, representing the northeast entrance gate). The northeast entrance gate will be revealed in more detail throughout the 2nd, and 3rd Chronicles))

*(Note15: If you look closely at the description of Revelation 7:2, you will notice another paradox when looking at the bold description of Job 2:1. For example: This description **'Then I saw another angel coming up from the east'** reveals the meaning behind this description **'and Satan also came with them to present himself before him'**))*

Here is the next clue: The **mighty angel** *(having the seal of the living God)* corresponds to the **7th golden lampstand** and represents the following **7th man**: **[Satan the 7th king]**!

*(Note16: This **mighty angel** corresponds to the 7th man (7th golden lampstand) and represents **Satan,** the mightiest angel of the seven as representing the mighty **7th king**, who defeated the other six kings who came before him. This revelation reveals the meaning behind the bold description 'But even the archangel Michael, when he was disputing with the devil about the body of Moses, **did not himself dare to condemn him for slander'** – Jude 9:9)*

The next thing you must do is bring back the base decoder regarding the 4th prominent horn and merge the revelations together into the correct place as seen below,

{4TH prominent horn} = [7TH head = 7TH hill = 7TH king] = [7th golden lampstand = 7th man] = [4TH beast = {beast coming out of the sea = ancient serpent *(Leviathan the serpent beast)*} = {scarlet beast = devil} = {red dragon *(iron teeth and bronze claws)*}] = [Satan *(name of a man)* = **Mighty Angel** *(coming up from the east)*] = [4th kingdom]

The next thing you must do is look closely at the bold portion in the following description of Zechariah 3:1.

[Then he showed me Joshua the high priest standing before the angel of the Lord, **and Satan standing at his right side to accuse him**]

(Note17: There is another major clue revealed by this description. For example: The name Joshua is symbolic and corresponds to a figure standing on the opposite side of Satan. This revelation will be revealed in more detail momentarily. The clue, however, is revealed by where Satan is standing or positioned to the throne to accuse Joshua. For example: if Satan is standing at Joshua's right, then Satan is standing at the left place of the throne))

Here is the next [vital clue]: The **Left place** has been prepared for the following king: [Satan the 7th king].

The next thing you must do is bring back the base decoder regarding the 4th prominent horn and merge the following place, which has been prepared for the 7th king into the correct place as seen below,

- {**Left place of the throne**} = [4TH prominent horn] = [7TH head = 7TH hill = 7TH king] = [7th golden lampstand = 7th man] = [4TH beast = {beast coming out of the sea = ancient serpent *(Leviathan the serpent beast)*} = {scarlet beast = devil} = {red dragon *(iron teeth and bronze claws)*}] = [Satan *(name of a man)* = Mighty angel *(coming up from the east)*] = [4th kingdom]

The right place is prepared for the following king

The next thing you must do is look closely at the bold portion in the following description of Revelation 5:6.

> **[Then I saw a Lamb, looking as if it had been slain, standing in the center of the throne,** encircled by the four living creatures and the elders. He had seven horns and seven eyes, which are the seven spirits of God sent out into all the earth.]

*(Note18: If you look closely at the bold part of the description of Revelation 5:6, you will notice another paradox when looking at the description of Ezekiel 9:2. For example: This description **'With them was a man clothed in linen who had a writing kit at his side. They came in and stood beside the bronze altar'** – Ezekiel 9:2, reveals a paradox to the following description **'Then I saw a Lamb, looking as if it had been slain, standing in the center of the throne'** - Revelation 5:6)*

To understand who the Lamb correspond to you must bring back the following revelations regarding the four great beasts as seen below,

- [1ST prominent horn] = [4TH head = 4TH hill = 4TH king] = [4th golden lampstand = 4th man] = [**1ST beast = lion**] = [1ST kingdom]

- {2^{ND} prominent horn} {2^{ND} prominent horn} = [5TH head = 5TH hill = 5TH king] = [5th golden lampstand = 5th man] = [**2ND beast = bear**] = [2ND kingdom]

- {3^{RD} prominent horn} = {3^{RD} prominent horn} = [6TH head = 6TH hill = 6TH king] = [6th golden lampstand = 6th man] = [**3RD beast = leopard**] = [3RD kingdom]

- [4TH prominent horn] = [7TH head = 7TH hill = 7TH king *(And he was given a great sword)*] = [7th golden lampstand = 7th man] = [4TH beast *(The beast and the ten horns you saw)* = **Beast coming out of the sea *(ancient serpent)* = Scarlet beast *(devil)* = Red dragon**] = [**Satan *(name of a man)*** = Mighty angel *(coming up from the east)* = Who is worthy to break the seals *and open the scroll? = Then I saw the beast and the kings of the earth and their armies gathered together to make war against the rider on the horse and his army]* = [4th kingdom]

*(Note19: If you look closely at the four great beasts that rose from the sea you will discover they also correspond to four living creatures standing around the throne. This revelation corresponds to the bold part of this description 'All the angels were standing around the throne and around the elders **and the four living creatures**' – Revelation 7:11)*

To understand this, you must bring back the revelation regarding the four great beasts and merge the four living creatures revealed from Revelation 4:7 in their proper places as seen below,

- [1ST prominent horn] = [4TH head = 4TH hill = 4TH king] = [4th golden lampstand = 4th man] = [1ST beast = lion = **1ST living creature = like a lion**] = [1ST kingdom]

- {2ND prominent horn} {2ND prominent horn} = [5TH head = 5TH hill = 5TH king] = [5th golden lampstand = 5th man] = [2ND beast = bear = **2ND living creature = like an ox**] = [2ND kingdom]

- {3RD prominent horn} = {3RD prominent horn} = [6TH head = 6TH hill = 6TH king] = [6th golden lampstand = 6th man] = [3RD beast = leopard = **3RD living creature = face like a man**] = [3RD kingdom]

- [4TH prominent horn] = [7TH head = 7TH hill = 7TH king *(And he was given a great sword)*] = [7th golden lampstand = 7th man] = [4TH beast *(The beast and the ten horns you saw)* = Beast coming out of the sea *(ancient serpent)* = Scarlet beast *(devil)* = Red dragon *(Satan)*] = [Satan *(name of a man)* = Mighty angel *(coming up from the east)* = Who is worthy to break the seals and open the scroll? = **4TH living creature = like a flying eagle** = Then I saw the beast and the kings of the earth and their armies gathered together to make war against the rider on the horse and his army] = [4th kingdom]

(Note20: If you recall from the previous revelations there also arose a mysterious 5th beast, which started small but grew in power. This 5th beast (as representing a 5th prominent horn), rose from the 4th beast (as representing a 4th prominent horn))

To understand this, bring back the revelations revealed by the 5th prominent horn and look closely at the 5th beast as seen below,

- [5th prominent horn] = [8th king *(And from His mouth proceeds a sharp sword)*] = [Someone like a son of man *(will hate the prostitute)* = Man clothed in linen *(writing kit at his side)* = He came and took the scroll from the right hand of him who sat on the throne! = The armies of heaven were following him, riding on white horses and dressed in fine linen, white and clean] = [Solid gold lampstand] = [**5th beast = Woman**]

*(Note21: This mysterious 5th beast also represents a 5th living creature and is also standing in the center of the throne in the presence of the four living creatures. This **5th living creature** also corresponds to the description **'the beast who once was, and now is not'** as well as the description **'someone like a son of man'**))*

To illustrate this, bring back the revelation regarding the 5th prominent horn and merge the **Lamb** with the **5th living creature** corresponding to the **5th beast** as seen below,

- [5th prominent horn] = [8th king *(And from His mouth proceeds a sharp sword)*] = [Someone like a son of man *(will hate the prostitute)* = Man clothed in linen *(writing kit at his side)* = He came and took the scroll from the right hand of him who sat on the throne! = The armies of heaven were following him, riding on white horses and dressed in fine linen, white and clean] = [Solid gold lampstand] = [5th beast = **5th living creature = Lamb looking as if slain** = Woman]

(Note22: Here, you can clearly see with your own eyes another deceptive lie that is believed and taught throughout Christianity of how the Lamb, looking as though slain represented Jesus. As you can see the evidence before you, the lamb represents a woman)

(Note23: The next step is to look closely at the description of Zechariah 3:1, to reveal another clue. This clue is revealed by the understanding as to where Joshua is standing or positioned before Satan the mighty angel)

Look again at the bold portion in the following description of Zechariah 3:1 below,

> [Then he showed me Joshua the high priest standing before the angel of the Lord, **and Satan standing at his right side to accuse him**]

*(Note24: Within this description reveals the next clue. For example: The name **Joshua** is symbolic and corresponds to the description **'someone like a son of man'**. Thus, it is not Joshua standing opposite Satan (7th golden lampstand), but 'someone like a son of man (solid gold lampstand).' This revelation reveals the paradox between the following three descriptions: **'and among the lampstands was someone like a son of man'** – Revelation 1:12, and this description **'and there before me was one like a son of man, coming with the clouds of heaven. He approached the Ancient of Days and was led into his presence'** – Daniel 7:13., reveals the meaning behind this description **'He went and took the scroll from the right hand of him who sat on the throne'** – Revelation 5:7)*

Here is the next clue: The **Right place** has been prepared for the following king: [Woman the 8th king].

The next thing you must do is bring back the base decoder regarding the 5th prominent horn and merge the revelation into the correct place as seen below,

- **{Right place of the throne}** = [5th prominent horn] = [Solid gold lampstand = Someone like a son of man = Man clothed in linen *(writing kit at his side)* = 8th king]] = [5th beast = Woman = 5th living creature = Lamb looking as if slain]

(Note25: The right and left places have been fulfilled concerning the 7th and 8th king. However, there is another clue hidden within the mystery that will catapult the understanding into the reason as to why these places have been prepared for Satan and the woman. This clue will be revealed behind the mystery of Satan's accusation! To uncover this mystery, you must begin by looking closely at the bold descriptions in the verses of Revelation 5:2 and 5:7)

The revelation revealed behind Satan's accusation

The next thing you must do is look closely at the bold portion in the following two descriptions of below,

Revelation 5:2 - [And I saw a mighty angel proclaiming in a loud voice, "**Who is worthy to break the seals and open the scroll?**" But no one in heaven or on earth or under the earth could open the scroll or even look inside it]

Revelation 5:7 - [**He came and took the scroll from the right hand of him who sat on the throne**]

Next, merge the two bold descriptions with their respective kings to reflect their respective places to the throne as seen below,

- **{Left side of the throne}** = [Satan *(name of a man)* = Mighty angel *(coming up from the east)* = ***Who is worthy to break the seals and open the scroll?***] = [4TH prominent horn] = [7TH head = 7TH hill = 7TH king] = [7th golden lampstand = 7th man] = [4TH beast = {beast coming out of the sea = ancient serpent *(Leviathan the serpent beast)*} = {scarlet beast = devil} = {red dragon *(iron teeth and bronze claws)*}] = 4th living creature = like a flying eagle] = [4th kingdom]

- **{Right side of the throne}** = [5th prominent horn] = [Solid gold lampstand = Someone like a son of man = Man clothed in linen *(writing kit at his side)* = ***He came and took the scroll from the right hand of him who sat on the throne!*** = 8th king] = [5th beast = Woman = 5th living creature = Lamb looking as if slain]

Here is the next clue. Bring back the revelations regarding the seven horns and look at the seven men.

- {Two horns *(ram)*} = [two heads = two hills = two kings] = [two golden lampstands = **1st and 2nd men**]

- {Larger horn *(goat)*} = [third head = third hill = 3RD king] = [golden lampstand = **3rd man**]

  - [1ST prominent horn] = [4TH head = 4TH hill = 4TH king] = [4th golden lampstand = **4th man**] = [1ST beast = lion = 1ST living creature = like a lion] = [1ST kingdom]

  - {2ND prominent horn} {2ND prominent horn} = [5TH head = 5TH hill = 5TH king] = [5th golden lampstand = **5th man**] = [2ND beast = bear = 2ND living creature = like an ox] = [2ND kingdom]

  - {3RD prominent horn} = {3RD prominent horn} = [6TH head = 6TH hill = 6TH king] = [6th golden lampstand = **6th man**] = [3RD beast = leopard = 3RD living creature = face like a man] = [3RD kingdom]

  - [4TH prominent horn] = [7TH head = 7TH hill = 7TH king *(And he was given a great sword)*] = [7th golden lampstand = **7th man**] = [4TH beast *(The beast and the ten horns you saw)* = Beast coming out of the sea *(ancient serpent)* = Scarlet beast *(devil)* = Red dragon *(Satan)*] = [Satan *(name of a man)* = Mighty angel *(coming up from the east)* = Who is worthy to break the seals and open the scroll? = 4TH living creature = like a flying eagle = Then I saw the beast and the kings of the earth and their armies gathered together to make war against the rider on the horse and his army] = [4th kingdom]

Here is the final clue: There was no man found throughout the heavenly realm who was worthy to break the seals and open the scroll.

Here is the **[final revelation]**: The accusation of Satan *(the mighty angel coming up from the east having the seal of the living God)* corresponds to the following description **'who is worthy to break the seals and open the scroll'** and represents the following revelation: [A woman was found to be worthier than all the men standing before the Ancient of Days]!

*(Note26: This revelation lays the foundation to understanding how this description '**The beast and the ten horns you saw will hate the prostitute**' - Revelation 17:16, will come to materialize. This revelation will be revealed in detail shortly)*

The beast and the ten horns

The next thing you must do is look closely at the following description of Revelation 17:16.

> [**The beast and the ten horns you saw will hate the prostitute**. They will bring her to ruin and leave her naked; they will eat her flesh and burn her with fire]

*(Note27: Within this description reveals two vital clues. The first step is to reveal the identity of the beast and the ten horns. For example: The **beast** and the **ten horns** represent a 4th beast (with ten horns). Thus, the 4th beast and ten horns (4th prominent horn) correspond to a 7th king (7th golden lampstand) and represents the mighty angel who comes up from the east having the seal of the living God in his hand))*

Here is the [1st vital clue]: The following description **'the beast and the ten horns you saw'** *(4th beast with ten horns)* represent the following name of the **mighty angel** who comes up from the east: [Satan the 7th man]!

The next thing you must do is bring back the base decoder regarding the 4th prominent horn and merge the bold description together in its proper place as seen below,

- {Left side of the throne} = [Satan *(name of a man)* = Mighty angel *(coming up from the east)* = Who is worthy to break the seals and open the scroll?] = [4TH prominent horn] = [7TH head = 7TH hill = 7TH king] = [7th golden lampstand = 7th man] = [4TH beast **(The beast and the ten horns you saw)** = {beast coming out of the sea = ancient serpent *(Leviathan the serpent beast)*} = {scarlet beast = devil} = {red dragon *(iron teeth and bronze claws)*}] = 4th living creature = like a flying eagle] = [4th kingdom]

The Prostitute

*(Note28: The second step is to reveal the identity of the prostitute. For example: The **prostitute** is symbolic and corresponds to the description '**someone like a son of man**' as representing the '**solid gold lampstand**'))*

Here is the [2nd vital clue]: The **prostitute** corresponds to the description **'someone like a son of man'** and represents the following gender: [Woman the 8th king]!

The next thing you must do is bring back the base decoder regarding the 5th prominent horn and merge the bold description together in its proper place as seen below,

- {Right side of the throne} = [5th prominent horn] = [Solid gold lampstand = Someone like a son of man = Man clothed in linen *(writing kit at his side)* = He came and took the scroll from the right hand of him who sat on the throne! = 8th king] = [5th beast = Woman = 5th living creature = Lamb looking as if slain *(will hate the prostitute)*]

The next thing you must do is look closely at the next two descriptions below,

- Revelation 19:19 - [Then I saw the beast and the kings of the earth and their armies gathered together to make war against the rider on the horse and his army]

- Revelation 19:14 - [The armies of heaven were following him, riding on white horses and dressed in fine linen, white and clean]

Next, merge the respective armies from the descriptions above together with their respective kings as seen below,

- {Left side of the throne} = [Satan *(name of a man)* = **Then I saw the beast and the kings of the earth and their armies gathered together to make war against the rider on the horse and his army** = Mighty angel *(coming up from the east)* = *Who is worthy to break the seals and open the scroll?*] = [4TH prominent horn] = [7TH head = 7TH hill = 7TH king] = [7th golden lampstand = 7th man] = [4TH beast *(The beast and the ten horns you saw)* = {beast coming out of the sea = ancient serpent *(Leviathan the serpent beast)*}] = {scarlet beast = devil} = {red dragon *(iron teeth and bronze claws)*}] = [4th living creature = like a flying eagle] = [4th kingdom]

- {Right side of the throne} = [5th prominent horn] = [Solid gold lampstand = Someone like a son of man = Man clothed in linen *(writing kit at his side)* = *He came and took the scroll from the right hand of him who sat on the throne!* = **The armies of heaven were following him, riding on white horses and dressed in fine linen, white and clean** = 8th king] = [5th beast = Woman = 5th living creature = Lamb looking as if slain *(will hate the prostitute)*]

(Note29: If you look closely at the following description **'Then I saw the beast and the kings of the earth and their armies'** *you will discover it too is symbolic. For example: this description* **'Then I saw the beast'** *corresponds to the* **4th beast**. *Example2: this description* **'and the kings of the earth'** *corresponds to the* **ten kings** *as representing the* **ten horns** *of the 4th beast. Therefore, the description is symbolic for representing the 4th beast and ten horns as Satan the 7th king)*

The preparation for war has commenced. The two remaining kings must now choose their weapons. The weapons they choose are revealed in the following two descriptions: Revelation 6:4 and Revelation 19:15.

Next, look closely at the bold portion in the following two descriptions below,

> Revelation 6:4 – [Then another horse went forth. It was fiery red, and its rider was granted permission to take peace from the earth and to make men slay one another. **And he was given a great sword**]

> Revelation 19:15 - [**And from His mouth proceeds a sharp sword** with which to strike down the nations]

The final thing you must do is merge the weapons together with their respective kings as seen below,

- {Left side of the throne} = [Satan *(name of a man)* = Then I saw the beast and the kings of the earth and their armies gathered together to make war against the rider on the horse and his army = Mighty angel *(coming up from the east)* = Who is worthy to break the seals and open the scroll?] = [4TH prominent horn] = [7TH head = 7TH hill = 7TH king ***(And he was given a great sword)***] = [7th golden lampstand = 7th man] = [4TH beast *(The beast and the ten horns you saw)* = {beast coming out of the sea = ancient serpent *(Leviathan the serpent beast)*} = {scarlet beast = devil} = {red dragon *(iron teeth and bronze claws)*}] = 4th living creature = like a flying eagle] = [4th kingdom]

- {Right side of the throne} = [5th prominent horn] = [Solid gold lampstand = Someone like a son of man = Man clothed in linen *(writing kit at his side)* = He came and took the scroll from the right hand of him who sat on the throne! = The armies of heaven were following him, riding on white horses and dressed in fine linen, white and clean = ***(And from His mouth proceeds a sharp sword)*** = 8th king] = [5th beast = Woman = 5th living creature = Lamb looking as if slain *(will hate the prostitute)*]

- The battle between the two kings begins! Which of them will become the King of Kings? -

King of Kings

The next thing you must do is look closely at the following description of Revelation 12:7.

> [Then war broke out in heaven. Michael and his angels fought against the dragon, and the dragon and his angels fought back]

(Note30: There are two vital clues revealed in this description. The first step is to understand the symbolic meaning of who the dragon corresponds to?)

To uncover this mystery, bring back the revelation revealed by the 4th prominent horn and look closely at the bold portion.

- [4TH prominent horn] = [7TH head = 7TH hill = 7TH king *(And he was given a great sword)*] = [7th golden lampstand = 7th man] = [4TH beast *(The beast and the ten horns you saw)* = Beast coming out of the sea *(ancient serpent)* = Scarlet beast *(devil)* = **Red dragon**] = [**Satan *(name of a man)* = Mighty angel** *(coming up from the east)* = *Who is worthy to break the seals and open the scroll?* = 4TH living creature = like a flying eagle = Then I saw the beast and the kings of the earth and their armies gathered together to make war against the rider on the horse and his army] = [4th kingdom]

Here is the [1st vital clue]: The **dragon** corresponds to the **red dragon** and represents the name of the following king: [Satan (the 7th king)].

*(Note31: The second step is to understand the symbolic meaning of who Michael corresponds to. For example: The name **Michael** is symbolic and corresponds to the description 'someone like a son of man'))*

Here is the [2nd vital clue]: The name **Michael** corresponds to the description **'Someone like a son of man'** and represents the gender of the following king: [Woman the 8th king].

{Important note… Michael does not fight against the red Dragon. The red dragon as previously revealed corresponds to Satan the 7th king. Thus, it is not the red dragon doing the fighting. It is Satan the mighty angel who represents the powerful 7th king that fights against the woman the 8th king}

The next thing you must do is bring back the base decoder regarding the 5th prominent horn and merge Michael in its respective place as seen below,

- [5th prominent horn] = [Solid gold lampstand = Someone like a son of man = **Michael** = Man clothed in linen *(writing kit at his side)* = He came and took the scroll from the right hand of him who sat on the throne! = The armies of heaven were following him, riding on white horses and dressed in fine linen, white and clean = *(And from His mouth proceeds a sharp sword)* = 8th king] = [5th beast = Woman = 5th living creature = Lamb looking as if slain *(will hate the prostitute)*]

The next thing you must do is look closely at the bold portion in the following description of Genesis 3:15.

> [**And I will put enmity between you and the woman**, and between your offspring and hers; **he will crush your head, and you will strike his heel**]

*(Note32: There is a major clue revealed within this description. To reveal the clue, you must start by looking closely at the bold word in the following description 'I will put <u>**enmity**</u> between you and the woman.' For example: The word (enmity) when used as a synonym represents the following meaning: **dislike, hatred, hostility, animosity, antagonism and antipathy** (Thus, representing **a deep-seated** or **deep-rooted dislike** for someone or something). This revelation reveals another paradox. Example2: The following description 'I will put enmity between you (as representing the serpent) **and the woman** (as representing Eve),' corresponds to the following description 'The beast and ten horns you saw (as representing Satan the 7th king) **will hate the prostitute** (as representing the woman as the 8th king))*

Look closely at the illustration below,

- Serpent = 4th beast = Satan the 7th king
- Eve = Prostitute = 5th beast = woman the 8th king

Here is the next clue. The **enmity** the serpent has against Eve corresponds to the **hatred** Satan has against the prostitute. The word **(enmity)** and **(hatred)** corresponds to the description **'who is worthy to break the seal and open the scroll.'** Thus, she was found to be more worthy than he!

(Note33: There are two vital clues also revealed in this description. For example: One of the kings will crush the head of the other; and one will strike the heel of the other)

To reveal the next vital clues, look closely at the following description of Psalm 74:14 below,

[It was you who crushed the heads of Leviathan and gave him as food to the creatures of the desert]

*(Note34: Leviathan is symbolic and corresponds to the following revelations: **[Beast coming out of the sea (ancient serpent) = Scarlet beast (devil) = Red dragon (Satan)]** as representing the 4th beast))*

Here is the [1st vital clue]: The following description **'he will crush your head'** *(as representing Eve)* corresponds to the **5th beast** *(as representing someone like a son of man)* and represents the gender of the following king: [Woman the 8th king].

Here is the [2nd vital clue]: The following description **'and you will strike his heel** *(as representing the serpent)***'** corresponds to the **4th beast** *(as representing Leviathan)* and represents the name of the following king: [Satan the 7th king].

{**Important Note...** The following description 'and you will strike his heel' is symbolic and reveals another paradox as corresponding to the accusation in which, Satan the mighty angel, brings against the woman by the following question 'who is worthy to break the seals and open the scroll.' Thus, the revelation of how Satan the 7th king, strikes the heel of the woman who represents the 8th king, is also revealed by the following revelations - **'the beast and the ten horns you saw** (4th beast as representing Satan the 7th king) **will hate the prostitute** (5th beast as representing the woman as the 8th king). The reason as to why Satan strikes the heel of the woman, is because she was found to be more worthy than he, the mighty 7th king, who represents the mightiest angel of the seven)}

The next thing you must do is bring back the revelation regarding the two remaining kings left from the previous equation known as The Process of Elimination. See below,

- [4TH prominent horn] = [7TH head = 7TH hill = 7TH king *(And he was given a great sword)*] = [7th golden lampstand = 7th man] = [4TH beast *(The beast and the ten horns you saw)* = {beast coming out of the sea = ancient serpent *(Leviathan the serpent beast)*} = {scarlet beast = devil} = {red dragon *(iron teeth and bronze claws)*}] = [Satan *(name of a man)* = Mighty angel *(coming up from the east)* = Who is worthy to break the seals and open the scroll? = 4th living creature = like a flying eagle = Then I saw the beast and the kings of the earth and their armies gathered together to make war against the rider on the horse and his army] = [4th kingdom]

- [5th prominent horn] = [Solid gold lampstand = Someone like a son of man = Michael = Man clothed in linen *(writing kit at his side)* = He came and took the scroll from the right hand of him who sat on the throne! = The armies of heaven were following him, riding on white horses and dressed in fine linen, white and clean = (And from His mouth proceeds a sharp sword) = 8th king] = [5th beast = Woman = 5th living creature = Lamb looking as if slain *(will hate the prostitute)*]

Next, subtract the {**4th prominent horn** *(as representing the 7th king)*} from the base decoder!

Here is the next clue: The **beast and ten horns** *(as corresponding to the 4th beast)*, who represents **Satan the 7th king**, has now fallen by the rise of the following king: [Woman the 8th king].

(Note34: The victory of the 8th king (someone like a son of man), who defeated the 7th king (as representing Satan the mighty angel) reveals the meaning behind the following description **'On his robe and on his thigh he has this name written: king of kings'** *– Revelation 19:16)*

The next thing you must do is bring back the base decoder regarding the 5th prominent horn and merge the revelation into the correct place as seen below,

- [5th prominent horn] = [Solid gold lampstand = Someone like a son of man = Michael = Man clothed in linen *(writing kit at his side)* = He came and took the scroll from the right hand of him who sat on the throne! = The armies of heaven were following him, riding on white horses and dressed in fine linen, white and clean = *(And from His mouth proceeds a sharp sword)* = 8th king = **King of Kings**] = [5th beast = Woman = 5th living creature = Lamb looking as if slain *(will hate the prostitute)*]

The next thing you must do is look closely at the bold description in the following verse of Luke 19:27.

- [**But those enemies of mine who did not want me to be king over them**—bring them here and kill them in front of me]

*(Note35: Within this description reveals another major clue. For example: This description does not correspond to Jesus. This part of the description '**But those enemies of mine who did not want me to be king over them**' is symbolic and corresponds to the seven horns revealed as the seven kings. And this part of the description '**—bring them here and kill them in front of me**' is also symbolic and corresponds to the 8th king (someone like a son of man), revealed as the woman. This revelation reveals the meaning behind the following description '**Out of one of them came another horn, which started small but grew in power**' - Daniel 8:9)*

The final thing you must do is look closely at the bold description in the verse of Revelation 19:12,

[His eyes are like blazing fire, and on his head are many crowns. **He has a name written on him that no one knows but he himself**]

(Note37: To solve this mystery, you must first locate a major clue within the description of Genesis 32:24–25)

'THE MYSTERY NAME REVEALED'

To begin, look closely at the bold description in verses of Genesis 32:24-25 below,

> **So Jacob was left alone, and a man wrestled with him till daybreak.** When the man saw that he could not overpower him, he touched the socket of Jacob's hip so that his hip was wrenched as he wrestled with the man]

(Note38: To reveal the name of the 8th king, you must reveal the name of the man who wrestles with Jacob. Hidden among the names of the eleven tribes of Israel reveals the clue. For example: One of the names listed among the tribes when translated in Hebrew means wrestler or one who wrestles))

Look closely at the following eleven tribes of Israel as seen below,

Ephraim	Asher	Dan	Simeon	Naphtali	
Reuben	Gad	Manasseh	Issachar	Zebulon	Benjamin

Next, separate the tribes to reflect their respective kingdoms born from the nations of Ephraim and Judah as seen below,

- {Nation of Ephraim} = [Ten tribes] = [**Ephraim, Asher, Dan, Simeon, Naphtali, Reuben, Gad, Manasseh, Issachar and Zebulon**] = {Kingdom of Samaria}

- {Nation of Judah} = [Single tribe] = [**Benjamin**] = {Kingdom of Jerusalem}

(Note39: As revealed previously, the tribe of Judah does not represent one of the tribes of Israel but does represent the name of a nation born from the tribe of Benjamin (Thus, the tribe of Benjamin emerges into the nation of Judah). This revelation brings the total number of tribes to eleven tribes (with one tribe missing). This revelation corresponds to the following description **'I will take the kingdom from his son's hands and give you ten tribes. I will give one tribe to his son'** *– 1st Kings 11:34-36))*

Next, separate the kingdoms to reflect their respective fathers as seen below,

- **{Descendants of Esau}** = [Ten Tribes: Ephraim, Asher, Dan, Simeon, Naphtali, Reuben, Gad, Manasseh, Issachar and Zebulon] = {Kingdom of Samaria}

- **{Descendants of Jacob}** = {Nation of Judah} = [Single Tribe: Benjamin] = {Kingdom of Jerusalem}

(Note40: Within the descendants of Esau reveals the name of a tribe that when translated in Hebrew translates to the words 'wrestler' or 'one who wrestles')

Here is the [vital clue]: The tribe that corresponds to the description **'and a man wrestled with him till daybreak'** represents the following name: [tribe of Naphtali]!

(Note41: The Hebrew translation for the name Naphtali means **'one who wrestles,'** *or* **'one that struggles or fights.'**)

Here is the [final revelation]: The following description **'He has a name written on him that no one knows but he himself'** corresponds to the following description **'someone like a son of man'** and represents the name of the 8th king: [Naphtali *(one that struggles or fights)*]!

(Note42: The name Naphtali is symbolic for representing one that struggles or fights. This revelation corresponds to the struggle and battle between the 8th king having overcame the mighty 7th king. This revelation reveals the meaning behind this description – **'Who is this coming from Edom, from Bozrah, with his garments stained crimson? Who is this, robed in splendor, striding forward in the greatness of his strength? "It is I** *(as representing the name Naphtali)*, **proclaiming victory, mighty to save'** *- Isaiah 63:1.)*

{Important note… This description **'with his garments stained crimson? Who is this, robed in splendor'** corresponds to the description **'and among the lampstands was someone like a son of man, dressed in a robe reaching down to his feet'** – Revelation 1:13 as well as the description **'With them was a man clothed in linen who had a writing kit at his side'** - Ezekiel 9:2. Thus, corresponding to the solid gold lampstand and representing the woman (5th living creature) as the triumphant, 8th king}

*(Note43: The 8th king descends from Esau. The reason she comes from Edom, from Bozrah is because Esau represents the father of Edom. This revelation corresponds to the description 'So Esau (that is, Edom) settled in the hill country of Seir. This is the account of the family line of Esau the father of the Edomites in the hill country of Seir - Genesis 36:8-9. This description **'Who is this coming from Edom'** reveals the revelation of how the description 'someone like a son of man' as representing Naphtali the 8th king (King of Kings), descends from Esau))*

{Important note... The name Naphtali is symbolic only and reveals the name behind the description 'someone like a son of man' who represents the 8th king. The name Naphtali does not represent the name of the woman. Her name will be revealed in detail in the later chapters}

The next thing you must do is bring back the base decoder regarding the 5th prominent horn and merge the revelation into its respective place as seen below,

- [5th prominent horn] = [Solid gold lampstand = Someone like a son of man = Michael = Man clothed in linen *(writing kit at his side)* = He came and took the scroll from the right hand of him who sat on the throne! = The armies of heaven were following him, riding on white horses and dressed in fine linen, white and clean = (And from His mouth proceeds a sharp sword) = 8th king = King of Kings = **Naphtali**] = [5th beast = Woman = 5th living creature = Lamb looking as if slain *(will hate the prostitute)*]

The final thing you must do is bring back the following revelation revealed by the symbolic numbers for both (woman) and (man), and merge the name of the 8th king in its respective place as seen below,

- [Symbolic number for Man] = [four it is man's number = 777] = [Satan the 7th king]

- [Symbolic number for Woman] = [**someone like a son of man** = 666] = [**Naphtali** the 8th king]

Congratulations!!! You have successfully completed the 2nd Chapter by revealing the true identity behind the title: King of Kings!

CHAPTER THREE- 1st PHASE OF THE CRYPTEX PUZZLE- REVELATION OF THE SIGN

In this chapter, the earth must prepare itself for the awaited hour. The hour of Judgement foreseen through the eyes of the prophet Daniel! A coming war, where the deeds of evil will be exposed in a hostel land! A final war, where the curtain of the fourth kingdom, which once hung as a unified banner over the City of David, will forever be torn apart!

*(Note: The hour of Judgement represents a final war that takes place in a hostel land. This revelation will reveal the true meaning behind the following description of Ephesians 6:12 – '**For our struggle is not against flesh and blood, but against the rulers, against the authorities, against the powers of this dark world**')*

The first thing you must do is look closely at the bold portion in the following description of Revelation 6:1.

> [**I watched as the Lamb opened the first of the seven seals**. Then I heard one of the four living creatures say in a voice like thunder, "Come!"]

(Note2: There is a major clue revealed by this description. To reveal the clue, you must open the sealed scroll. To open the scroll, you must bring back the base decoder and merge the seven broken seals together with the description of Matthew 23:13-33)

Next, break the seals and **OPEN** the scroll!

THE SCROLL REVEALED

{1st broken seal} - **{2nd broken seal}** = {Two horns *(ram)*} = [two heads = two hills = two kings] = [two golden lampstands = 1st and 2nd men]:

- [Woe to you, teachers of the law and Pharisees, you hypocrites! You shut the kingdom of heaven in men's faces. You yourselves do not enter, nor will you let those enter who are trying to]

- [Woe to you, teachers of the law and Pharisees, you hypocrites! You travel over land and sea to win a single convert, and when he becomes one, you make him twice as much a son of hell as you are]

{3rd broken seal} = {Larger horn *(goat)*} = [third head = third hill = 3RD king] = [3rd golden lampstand = 3rd man]:

- [Woe to you, blind guides! You say, 'If anyone swears by the temple, it means nothing; but if anyone swears by the gold of the temple, he is bound by his oath.' You blind fools! Which is greater: the gold, or the temple that makes the gold sacred? You also say, 'If anyone swears by the altar, it means nothing; but if anyone swears by the gift on it, he is bound by his oath.' You blind men! Which is greater: the gift, or the altar that makes the gift sacred? Therefore, he who swears by the altar swears by it and by everything on it. And he who swears by the temple –swears by it and by the one who dwells in it. And he who swears by heaven swears by God's throne and by the one who sits on it]

{4th broken seal} = {1ST prominent horn} = [4TH head = 4TH hill = 4TH king] = [4th golden lampstand = 4th man]:

- [Woe to you, teachers of the law and Pharisees, you hypocrites! You give a tenth of your spices- mint, dill and cumin. But you have neglected the more important matters of the law-justice, mercy and faithfulness. You should have practiced the latter, without neglecting the former. You blind guides! You strain out a gnat but swallow a camel]

{5th **broken seal**} = {2ND prominent horn} = [5TH head = 5TH hill = 5TH king] = [5th golden lampstand = 5th man]:

- [Woe to you, teachers of the law and Pharisees, you hypocrites! You clean the outside of the cup and dish, but inside they are full of greed and self-indulgence. Blind Pharisee! First clean the inside of the cup and dish, and then the outside also will be clean]

{6th **broken seal**} = {3RD prominent horn} = [6TH head = 6TH hill = 6TH king] = [6th golden lampstand = 6th man]:

- [Woe to you, teachers of the law and Pharisees, you hypocrites! You are like whitewashed tombs, which look beautiful on the outside but on the inside are full of dead men's bones and everything unclean. In the same way, on the outside you appear to people as righteous but on the inside you are full of hypocrisy and wickedness]

{7th **broken seal**} = [4TH prominent horn] = [7TH head = 7TH hill = 7TH king] = [7th golden lampstand = 7th man]:

- [Woe to you, teachers of the law and Pharisees, you hypocrites! You build tombs for the prophets and decorate the greaves of the righteous. And you say, 'If we had lived in the days of our forefathers, we would not have taken part with them in shedding the blood of the prophets.' So you testify against yourselves that you are the descendants of those who murdered the prophets. Fill up, then, the measure of the sin of your forefathers! You snakes! You brood of vipers! How will you escape being condemned to hell?]

*(Note3: Each of the **seven broken seals** represent a judgement against each of the seven golden lampstands as representing seven men. All of which correspond to seven horns that are seven heads and seven hills, on which the woman sits. Thus, representing seven kings. The **seven spoken judgements** that are seven woes as revealed in the description of Matthew 23:13-33, reveals the meaning behind this description **'And from His mouth proceeds a sharp sword with which to strike down the nations'** – Revelation 19:15. There is a vital clue revealed in the description of Zechariah 5:2-3.)*

Look closely at the following description of Zechariah 5:2-3 below,

> [He asked me, "What do you see?" I answered, "I see a flying scroll, twenty cubits long and ten cubits wide." And he said to me, "This is the curse that is going out over the whole land; for according to what it says on one side, every thief will be banished, and according to what it says on the other, everyone who swears falsely will be banished]

(Note4: The breaking of the 'seven seals' corresponding to the 'seven woes' represents a curse that is going out over the whole land. The question is which lands. The flying cursed scroll has two sides that will be revealed in two parts, which will affect the 4th kingdom of Clay. This revelation will reveal the meaning behind the bold parts of the following descriptions **'for according to what it says on one side, every thief will be banished'** *(as corresponding to the Kingdom of Samaria (ten tribes)). And the following description* **'according to what it says on the other, everyone who swears falsely will be banished'** *(as corresponding to the Nation of Judah (single tribe that remained in the city)). This revelation will reveal the true meaning behind the following description 'Out of his mouth comes a sharp sword with which to strike down the nations' – Revelation 19:15)*

Here is the [vital clue]: The **scroll sealed with seven broken seals** *(Revelation 6:1-17)* correspond to **seven woes** *(Matthew 23:13-33)* and represents a **flying cursed scroll** *(Zechariah 5:1-3)* that is going out over the following two nations that had emerged from the 4th Kingdom of Clay, The City of David: [Nation of Judah] and [Kingdom of Samaria]

{Important note: To understand how the revelations will unfold, you must return to the 4th Kingdom of Clay}

Welcome to the City of David!

THE CITY OF DAVID

The first thing you must do is bring back the following description of Ezekiel 9:1, and look closely at the bold portion of the description below,

> [Then I heard him call out in a loud voice, **"Bring the guards of the city here, each with a weapon in his hand."** And I saw six men coming from the direction of the upper gate, which faces north, each with a deadly weapon in his hand]

*(Note5: Within this description reveals another major clue. To reveal the clue, you must first exit the threshing floor and cross the Bridge of Verses! Keep in mind the following revelation that **Four prominent horns** correspond to **Four great beasts**)*

THE BRIDGE of VERSES

1- [**Four prominent horns**] corresponds to [Four great beasts - *each different from the others, came up out of the sea - Daniel 7:3*]

2- [**Four great beasts**] corresponds to [Four living creatures - *standing before the throne - Revelation 4:7*]

3- [**Four living creatures**] correspond to [cherubims - *Ezekiel 10:15*]

4- [**Cherubims**] correspond to [Four chariots - *positioned in the sky - Zechariah 6:1-3*]

5- [**Four chariots**] correspond to [Four directions - *Zechariah 6:6*]

- Black horses toward the North Country, white horses toward the west and dappled horses toward the south. *(Note: the fiery red horses remain in the east)*

6- [**Four directions** - *north, west, south and east*] correspond to [four spirits - *Zechariah 6:5*]

- These are the four spirits of heaven, going out from standing in the presence of the Lord of the whole world.

7- [**Four spirits**] correspond to [Four angels - *Revelation 7:1-2*]

- After this I saw four angels standing at the four corners of the earth, holding back the four winds of the earth

8- [**Four angels**] correspond to [Four apocalyptic riders - *Revelation 6:1-8*]

- **White horse** *(Its rider held a bow)*, **fiery red one** *(Its rider was given power to take peace from the earth)*, **black horse** *(Its rider was holding a pair of scales in his hand)*, and **pale horse** *(Its rider was named Death)*.

Here is the next clue: The **guards of the city** *(each with a weapon in his hand)*, corresponds to the **four angels** that are **four spirits**, as well as **four living creatures** and represents the following riders: [Four apocalyptic riders]!

The next thing you must do is bring back the base decoder and merge the revelations revealed by the Bridge of Verses with their respective prominent horns as seen below,

- [1ST prominent horn] = [4TH head = 4TH hill = 4TH king] = [4th golden lampstand = 4th man] = [1ST beast = lion = **1ST living creature = like a lion = 1ST cherubim = 1ST chariot = 1ST spirit = 1ST angel = 1ST guard of the city = 1ST apocalyptic rider *(Its rider held a bow)***] = [1ST kingdom]

- {2^{ND} prominent horn} {2^{ND} prominent horn} = [5TH head = 5TH hill = 5TH king] = [5th golden lampstand = 5th man] = [2ND beast = bear = **2ND living creature = like an ox = 2ND cherubim = 2ND chariot = 2ND spirit = 2ND angel = 2ND guard of the city = 2ND apocalyptic rider *(Its rider was holding a pair of scales in his hand)***] = [2ND kingdom]

- {3^{RD} prominent horn} = {3^{RD} prominent horn} = [6TH head = 6TH hill = 6TH king] = [6th golden lampstand = 6th man] = [3RD beast = leopard = **3RD living creature = face like a man = 3RD cherubim = 3RD chariot = 3RD spirit = 3RD angel = 3RD guard of the city = 3RD apocalyptic rider *(to kill by sword, famine and plague)***] = [3RD kingdom]

- [4TH prominent horn] = [7TH head = 7TH hill = 7TH king *(And he was given a great sword)*] = [7th golden lampstand = 7th man] = [4TH beast *(The beast and the ten horns you saw)* = Beast coming out of the sea *(ancient serpent)* = Scarlet beast *(devil)* = Red dragon *(Satan)*] = [Satan *(name of a man)* = Mighty angel *(coming up from the east)* = Who is worthy to break the seals and open the scroll? = **4TH living creature = like a flying eagle = 4TH cherubim = 4TH chariot = 4TH spirit = 4TH angel = 4TH guard of the city = 4TH apocalyptic rider *(To him was given a large sword)***] = [Then I saw the beast and the kings of the earth and their armies gathered together to make war against the rider on the horse and his army] = [4th kingdom]

*(Note6: The fourth chariot (**fiery red horses** remain in the east sky) corresponds to the 4th apocalyptic rider (**fiery red** horses) and represents the **red dragon** as Satan, the mighty angel, who come up from the east possessing the seal of the living God))*

(Note7: Hidden within the revelation of the four guards of the city that are four living creatures as well as four chariot horses as representing four apocalyptic horses lies a great deception. For example: The great deception is revealed by the colors of the four chariot horses and the four apocalyptic horses.)

To uncover the mystery, you must bring back the following revelations regarding the colors of the four apocalyptic horses *(**Revelation 6:2-8**)* and the colors of the four chariot horses *(**Zechariah 6:2**)*

Look closely at the bold portions in the two descriptions of Revelation and Zechariah as seen below,

Revelation 6:2-8
- {The four apocalyptic horses *(Revelation)*} = [**white horse** – fiery red horse – pale horse – black horse]

Zechariah 6:2
- {The four chariot horses *(Zechariah)*} = [red chariot horses – black chariot horses – **white chariot horses** – dappled chariot horses]

(Note8: The first deception is revealed by the white chariot horses and the white apocalyptic horse. For example: These white horses do not correspond to the description 'I saw heaven standing open and there before me was a white horse, whose rider is called Faithful and True. With justice he judges and wages war' – Revelation 19:11)

To further understand this, you must cross-out the [white chariot horses] as well as the [white apocalyptic horse]

Revelation 6:2-8
- {The four apocalyptic horses *(Revelation)*} = [~~white horse~~ – fiery red horse – pale horse – black horse]

Zechariah 6:2
- {The four chariot horses *(Zechariah)*} = [red chariot horses – black chariot horses – ~~white chariot horses~~ – dappled chariot horses]

*(Note9: The next deception is revealed by the following revelation. The **'dappled chariot horses'** correspond to one of the apocalyptic horses, and the **'pale apocalyptic horse'** corresponds to the chariot horses)*

To understand this, you must merge the colored horses in the correct order corresponding to their respective places,

Revelation 6:2-8
- {Four apocalyptic horses *(Revelation)*} = [~~white horse~~ *(dappled chariot horses)* – fiery red horse – pale horse – black horse]

Zechariah 6:2
- {Four chariot horses *(Zechariah)*} = [red chariot horses – black chariot horses – ~~white chariot horses~~ *(pale horse)* – dappled chariot horses]

*(Note10: If you look closely, you will see how the **'white apocalyptic horse'** - Revelation 6:2, corresponds to the **'dappled chariot horses'** - Zechariah 6:3. And the **'white chariot horses'** - Zechariah 6:3, corresponds to the **'pale horse'** - Revelation 6:8)*

Next, remove the white apocalyptic horse and the white chariot horses from both descriptions and merge the colored horses in the correct order corresponding to their respective places.

Revelation 6:2-8
- {Four apocalyptic hoses *(Revelation)*} = [**dappled chariot horses** – fiery red horse – pale horse – black horse]

Zechariah 6:2
- {Four chariot horses *(Zechariah)*} = [red chariot horses – black chariot horses – **pale chariot horse** – dappled chariot horses]

*(Note11: The next deception is revealed behind the mystery of the **dappled horses**. For example: There is a hidden clue that reveals the true color of the dappled horses? To reveal this mystery, you must locate another major clue revealed in the description of Zechariah 1:8)*

Look closely at the bold portion in the description of Zechariah 1:8 below,

[During the night I had a vision, and **there before me was a man mounted on a red horse. He was standing among the myrtle trees in a ravine. Behind him were red, brown and white horses**]

(Note12: If you look closely at this description, you will notice where the clue is visible in plain sight. For example: If you carefully examine the following two descriptions **'there before me was a man mounted on a red horse'** *and* **'Behind him were red'** *you will discover it is incorrect (the horses are the same color). Example2: You will also notice that one of the color's* **(black horses)** *is not revealed within the description! You will also take note that the* **'white horses'** *does not belong in the description, which means it corresponds to the* **'pale horse'** *which is also not revealed in the description. Example3: One of the* **red horses** *corresponds to the missing* **black horse**. *Therefore, this description* **'Behind him were red'** *should be written as the following:* **'Behind him were black.'** *To reveal the true color of the dappled horses, you must merge the following two colors* **red** *(as seen in the description) and* **black** *(not seen in the description) to reveal the true color of the dappled horse)*

Here is the next clue: The true color of the dappled horse represents the following color: [Brown horse].

Next, remove the dappled apocalyptic horse and the dappled chariot horses from both descriptions and merge the brown horses in the correct places.

- {Four apocalyptic hoses *(Revelation)*} = [**Brown horse** – fiery red horse – pale horse – black horse]

- {Four chariot horses *(Zechariah)*} = [red chariot horses – black chariot horses – pale chariot horse –**Brown horses**]

*(Note13: By merging the two colors, '**red**' and '**black**' you will discover that '**brown**' is the true color of the dappled horses. This revelation reveals the '**brown horse**' to represent the 1st chariot horse as well as the 1st apocalyptic horse)*

The next thing you must do is bring back the base decoder regarding the four prominent horns and merge the revelations together regarding their respective colors in the correct places as seen below,

- {1ST prominent horn} = [4TH head = 4TH hill = 4TH king] = [4th star = 4th spirit before his throne = 4th angel blasting 4th trumpet] = [4th priest *(blowing trumpet)* = Harps = 4th man = 4th elder of Judah = 4th golden lampstand] = [1ST beast = lion = 1ST living creature = 1ST cherubim = 1ST chariot = **Brown horses** = 1ST spirit = 1ST angel = 1ST guard of the city = 1ST apocalyptic rider *(Its rider held a bow)* = **Brown horses**] = [1ST kingdom]

- {2ND prominent horn} = [5TH head = 5TH hill = 5TH king] = [5th star = 5th spirit before his throne = 5th angel blasting 5th trumpet] = [5th priest *(blowing trumpet)* = cymbals = 5th man = 5th elder of Judah = 5th golden lampstand] = [2ND beast = bear = 2ND living creature = 2ND cherubim = 2ND chariot = **Black horses** = 2ND spirit = 2ND angel = 2ND guard of the city = 2ND apocalyptic rider *(Its rider was holding a pair of scales in his hand)* = **Black horses**] = [2ND kingdom]

- {3RD prominent horn} = [6TH head = 6TH hill = 6TH king] = [6th star = 6th spirit before his throne = 6th angel blasting 7th trumpet] = [6th priest *(blowing trumpet)* = Lyres = 6th man = 6th elder of Judah = 6th golden lampstand] = [3RD beast = leopard = 3RD living creature = 3RD cherubim = 3RD chariot = **Pale horses** = 3RD spirit = 3RD angel = 3RD guard of the city = 3RD apocalyptic rider *(to kill by sword, famine and plague)* = **Pale horses**] = [3RD kingdom]

- {4TH prominent horn} = [7TH head = 7TH hill = 7TH king] = [7th star = 7th spirit before his throne = 7th angel blasting 7th trumpet] = [7th priest *(blowing trumpet)* = shouts = 7th man = 7th elder of Judah = 7th golden lampstand] = [Satan] = [4TH beast *(The beast and the ten horns you saw)* = Beast coming out of the sea *(ancient serpent)* = Scarlet beast *(devil)* = Red dragon *(Satan)*] = [Satan *(coming from the direction of the upper gate which faces north)* = Mighty angel *(coming up from the east)* = Who is worthy to break the seals and open the scroll? = 4TH living creature = 4TH cherubim = 4TH chariot = **Fiery red horses** = 4TH spirit = 4TH angel = 4TH guard of the city = 4TH apocalyptic rider *(To him was given a large sword)* = **Fiery red horses**] = [Then I saw the beast and the kings of the earth and their armies gathered together to make war against the rider on the horse and his army = And he was given a great sword] = [4th kingdom]

The next thing you must do is bring back the following description of Ezekiel 9:2, and look closely at the bolded portion in the description below,

[**With them was a man clothed in linen who had a writing kit at his side.** They came in and stood beside the bronze altar]

(Note14: Within this description reveals another hidden clue. For example: The six men, including Satan, the mighty angel, as representing the 7th man, correspond to seven heads and seven hills on which the woman sits. Thus, representing seven kings. They also correspond to seven golden lampstands. However, the 'man clothed in linen' does not represent the 7th man. This figure 'a man clothed in linen' is symbolic and corresponds to the description 'and among the lampstands was someone like a son of man', as representing the 8th king. Thus, it also corresponds to the 'solid gold lampstand'. Therefore, the man clothed in linen also corresponds to the following: a 5th beast, a 5th cherubim, a 5th chariot, a 5th spirit, and a 5th angel)

Here is the next clue: The **man clothed in linen** corresponds to the description **'someone like a son of man'** and represents the following guard: [a 5th Guard of the city]!

The next thing you must do is bring back the base decoder regarding the 5th prominent horn and merge the revelations together regarding the 5th beast as seen below,

- [5th prominent horn] = [Solid gold lampstand = Someone like a son of man = Man clothed in linen (writing kit at his side) = *He came and took the scroll from the right hand of him who sat on the throne!* = *The armies of heaven were following him, riding on white horses and dressed in fine linen, white and clean* = *(And from His mouth proceeds a sharp sword)* = 8th king = King of Kings = Naphtali] = [5th beast = Woman = 5th living creature = Lamb looking as if slain *(will hate the prostitute)* = **5th cherubim = 5th chariot = 5th spirit = 5th angel = 5th guard of the city**]

Next, look closely at the bolded portion in the following description of Revelation 19:11 below,

[I saw heaven standing open **and there before me was a white horse, whose rider is called Faithful and True.** With justice he judges and wages war]

*(Note15: The **white horse** as revealed in Revelation 19:11 (there before me was a white horse, whose rider is called Faithful and True), does not correspond to the **white apocalyptic horse** as revealed in Revelation 6:2 (I looked, and there before me was a white horse! Its rider held a bow))*

*(Note16: The '**white horse**' is symbolic and corresponds to a **5th living creature** as also representing a **5th guard of the city**. Thus, the 'rider' on the white horse is also symbolic and corresponds to the description 'someone like a son of man')*

Here is the next clue: The '**white horse**' corresponds to the '**5th living creature**' as well as the '**5th guard of the city**' and represents the following apocalyptic horse: [a 5th apocalyptic rider]!

The next thing you must do is bring back the base decoder regarding the 5th prominent horn and merge the revelations in its respective places as seen below,

- [5th prominent horn] = [Solid gold lampstand = Someone like a son of man = Man clothed in linen (writing kit at his side) = *He came and took the scroll from the right hand of him who sat on the throne! = The armies of heaven were following him, riding on white horses and dressed in fine linen, white and clean =* (And from His mouth proceeds a sharp sword) = 8th king = King of Kings = Lord of Lords = Naphtali] = [5th beast = Woman = 5th living creature = Lamb looking as if slain *(will hate the prostitute)* = 5th cherubim = 5th chariot = **White horse** = 5th spirit = 5th angel = 5th guard of the city = **5th apocalyptic rider *(from His mouth proceeds a sharp sword)* = White horse**]

The next thing you must do is look closely at the bolded portion in the following description of Revelation 8:5.

[Then the angel took the censer, filled it with fire from the altar, and hurled it on the earth; and there came **peals of thunder, rumblings, flashes of lightning and an earthquake**]

(Note17: Within this description reveals another major clue. For example: The following phenomenon's are also symbolic and correspond to the four spirits (as representing four angels positioned in the sky), as well as four chariots (as representing four living creatures). Thus, they also correspond to four guards of the city))

Here is the next clue: The following phenomenon's **'peals of thunder, rumblings, flashes of lightning and an earthquake'** corresponds to **'four guards of the city'** and represents the following apocalyptic riders: [Four apocalyptic riders].

Next, merge the revelations regarding the four phenomenon's together with their respective places as seen below,

- $\{1^{ST}$ prominent horn$\}$ = [4TH head = 4TH hill = 4TH king] = [4th star = 4th spirit before his throne = 4th angel blasting 4th trumpet] = [4th priest *(blowing trumpet)* = Harps = 4th man = 4th elder of Judah = 4th golden lampstand] = [1ST beast = lion = 1ST living creature = 1ST cherubim = 1ST chariot = Brown horses = 1ST spirit = 1ST angel = 1ST guard of the city = 1ST apocalyptic rider *(Its rider held a bow)* = **Peals of thunder** = Brown horses] = [1ST kingdom]

- $\{2^{ND}$ prominent horn$\}$ = [5TH head = 5TH hill = 5TH king] = [5th star = 5th spirit before his throne = 5th angel blasting 5th trumpet] = [5th priest *(blowing trumpet)* = cymbals = 5th man = 5th elder of Judah = 5th golden lampstand] = [2ND beast = bear = 2ND living creature = 2ND cherubim = 2ND chariot = Black horses = 2ND spirit = 2ND angel = 2ND guard of the city = 2ND apocalyptic rider *(Its rider was holding a pair of scales in his hand)* = **Rumblings** = Black horses] = [2ND kingdom]

- {3^RD prominent horn} = [6TH head = 6TH hill = 6TH king] = [6th star = 6th spirit before his throne = 6th angel blasting 7th trumpet] = [6th priest *(blowing trumpet)* = Lyres = 6th man = 6th elder of Judah = 6th golden lampstand] = [3RD beast = leopard = 3RD living creature = 3RD cherubim = 3RD chariot = Pale horses = 3RD spirit = 3RD angel = 3RD guard of the city = 3RD apocalyptic rider *(to kill by sword, famine and plague)* = **Flashes of lightning** = Pale horses] = [3RD kingdom]

- {4^TH prominent horn} = [7TH head = 7TH hill = 7TH king] = [7th star = 7th spirit before his throne = 7th angel blasting 7th trumpet] = [7th priest *(blowing trumpet)* = shouts = 7th man = 7th elder of Judah = 7th golden lampstand] = [Satan] = [4TH beast *(The beast and the ten horns you saw)* = Beast coming out of the sea *(ancient serpent)* = Scarlet beast *(devil)* = Red dragon *(Satan)*] = [Satan *(coming from the direction of the upper gate which faces north)* = Mighty angel *(coming up from the east)* = Who is worthy to break the seals and open the scroll? = 4TH living creature = 4TH cherubim = 4TH chariot = Fiery red horses = 4TH spirit = 4TH angel = 4TH guard of the city = 4TH apocalyptic rider *(To him was given a large sword)* = **Earthquake** = Fiery red horses] = [Then I saw the beast and the kings of the earth and their armies gathered together to make war against the rider on the horse and his army = And he was given a great sword] = [4th kingdom]

Next, look closely at the bolded portion in the following description of Revelation 11:19,

[Then God's temple in heaven was opened, and within his temple was seen the ark of his covenant. And there came flashes of lightning, rumblings, peals of thunder, an earthquake **and a great hailstorm**]

(Note18: Within this description reveals another major clue. For example: This phenomenon is also symbolic and corresponds to a 5th spirit, as representing a 5th angel as well as, a 5th chariot as also representing a 5th living creature. Therefore, this phenomenon represents a 5th guard of the city))

Here is the next clue: This phenomenon **'a great hailstorm'** corresponds to a **'fifth guard of the city'** and represents the following rider: [5th apocalyptic rider].

The next thing you must do is bring back the base decoder regarding the 5th prominent horn and merge the revelations in its respective place as seen below,

- [5th prominent horn] = [Solid gold lampstand = Someone like a son of man = Man clothed in linen (writing kit at his side) = *He came and took the scroll from the right hand of him who sat on the throne! = The armies of heaven were following him, riding on white horses and dressed in fine linen, white and clean = (And from His mouth proceeds a sharp sword)* = 8th king = King of Kings = Lord of Lords = Naphtali] = [5th beast = Woman = 5th living creature = Lamb looking as if slain *(will hate the prostitute)* = 5th cherubim = 5th chariot = White horse = 5th spirit = 5th angel = 5th guard of the city = 5th apocalyptic rider *(from His mouth proceeds a sharp sword)* = **A great hailstorm** = White horse]

THE FALL OF THE NATION OF JUDAH (The City of David)

The next thing you must do is look carefully at the bolded portion in the following description of Ezekiel 9:3-4.

> [Now the glory of the God of Israel went up from above the cherubim, where it had been, and moved to the threshold of the temple. Then the Lord called to the man clothed in linen who had the writing kit at his side and said to him, **"Go throughout the city of Jerusalem** and put a mark on the foreheads of those who grieve and lament over all the detestable things that are done in it]

(Note19: This description is structurally written deceptively and reveals another major clue! For example: The name of the city (not referring to the Holy City, called Jerusalem) corresponds to the original name of the city that resided within the City of David but renamed by the tribe of Benjamin (who remained in the City of David after the Kingdom was torn from King Solomon). If you recall, the city of Jerusalem (from the Kingdom of Jerusalem) will not emerge until after the second exodus period. However, this ancient city corresponds to the description 'the city where I chose to put my name' – 1st Kings 11:36. The clue, is revealed behind the understanding of the description written in Revelation 16:16 – 'Then they gathered the kings together to the place that in Hebrew is called Armageddon'. This revelation will be revealed in detail momentarily. Within one of the following two nations (the nation of Ephraim) or (the nation of Judah), will reveal the true name of the city.)

Next, look closely at the description of Revelation 16:16 below,

> [Then they gathered the kings together to the place that in Hebrew is called Armageddon]

*(Note20: The word Armageddon when translated in Greek means the following: **the site or time of a final and conclusive battle between the forces of good and evil**. Thus, the word Armageddon when translated in Hebrew represents the following meaning: **a place or region of a particular land, where the battle between the forces of good and evil will be fought**. Thus, the Greek translation for 'Armageddon' will correspond to what will happen within the city. And the Hebrew translation will correspond to the region within the city where it will take place)*

Here is the next [vital clue]: The following description **'Go throughout the city of Jerusalem'** corresponds to the description **'the city where I chose to put my name'** and represents the following city that reside within the Nation of Judah: [The ancient city called Megiddo]!

(Note21: The Hebrew translation for the Greek word Armageddon is Megiddo (meaning a place or region of a particular land). The following description 'the city where I chose to put my name' corresponds to the ancient city called Megiddo (resides in the land of Judah). Thus, the context regarding the previous description 'Go throughout the city of Jerusalem' is incorrect! The correct context refers to the following: **'Go throughout the city of Megiddo.'** *This revelation also reveals another deceptive trap within the Bible. For example: the city of Megiddo does not appear in the books of 1st and 2nd Kings, nor 1st and 2nd Chronicles as representing the city that resided within the Nation of Judah. The text refers to* **Jerusalem** *as the city. However, this is incorrect! The city of Jerusalem (also known as the Holy City) will emerge from within the Kingdom of Jerusalem. The Kingdom of Jerusalem will not emerge until after the 2nd exodus period, when the Nation of Judah comes out of captivity under Babylon after the rise of the Persian Empire. The Nation of Judah will first return to the land from which they were taken. This revelation corresponds to the following description "When I bring them back from captivity, the people in the land of Judah and in its towns will once again use these words: 'The LORD bless you, you prosperous city, you sacred mountain' – Jeremiah 31:23. From there, the Nation of Judah will move on to emerge into the Kingdom of Jerusalem. Thus, the nation of Judah will no longer reside in the land of the east but will settle in the land of the west, otherwise known as the land of the western hill country and will border the land of Egypt. It is here where the descendants of Judah will build the Holy City called Jerusalem. This revelation is revealed by the following description 'When they had gone, an angel of the Lord appeared to Joseph in a dream. "Get up," he said, "take the child and his mother and escape to Egypt' – Matthew 2:13. Therefore, the name Jerusalem should not appear in any of the books referring to the old testaments because those books only correspond to the 1st exodus period. The following books, Matthew, Mark, Luke and John will correspond to the second exodus period. This revelation will be revealed in more detail in the following title, The Elijah Doctrine2 (The Path of the Sign))*

The next thing you must do is look closely at the bolded portion in the following description of Ezekiel 9:3-4.

[Now the glory of the God of Israel went up from above the cherubim, where it had been, and moved to the threshold of the temple. Then the Lord called to the man clothed in linen who had the writing kit at his side and said to him, "Go throughout the city of Jerusalem and **put a mark on the foreheads of those who grieve and lament** over all the detestable things that are done in it]

(Note22: Within the bold description reveals another major clue. For example: Only males during this era (referring to the Age of Ram) partook in the practicing of baring the mark on their foreheads! The clue is revealed in the description of Exodus 4:25))

Look closely at the following description of Exodus 4:25 below,

[But Zipporah took a flint knife, cut off her son's foreskin and touched Moses feet with it]

Here is the next clue: The **mark on the foreheads** corresponds to the **removal of foreskin** and represents the following ancient practice: [The Ceremonial purification of circumcision].

(Note23: This ancient practice known as the ceremonial purification of circumcision represents the removal of foreskin from the male phallus (also known as circumcising the head of the male penis). This revelation reveals the meaning behind the following description 'On the eighth day the boy is to be circumcised' – Leviticus 12:3)

(Note24: The following description 'those who grieve and lament' reveals another major clue! For example: Only the descendants of Aaron grieve and lament. To reveal the next clue, you must locate a hidden clue revealed within the following two descriptions of 2nd Kings and 2nd Chronicles)

*(Note25: There is also a vital clue revealed behind the following description **'over all the detestable things that are done in it.'** This revelation will be revealed in more detail shortly!)*

Look closely at the bold portion in the following two descriptions below,

- 2nd KINGS 15:1-2 - [In the twenty-seventh year of Jeroboam king of Israel, **Azariah son of Amaziah king of Judah began to reign. He was sixteen years old when he became king, and he reigned in Jerusalem fifty-two years. His mother's name was Jecoliah**; she was from Jerusalem]

- 2nd CHRONICLES 26:1-3 - [Then all the people of Judah took **Uzziah, who was sixteen years old, and made him king in place of his father Amaziah.** He was the one who rebuilt Elath and restored it to Judah after Amaziah rested with his fathers. **Uzziah was sixteen years old when he became king, and he reigned in Jerusalem fifty-two years. His mother's name was Jecoliah**; she was from Jerusalem]

Next, remove the bold portion of the descriptions from the verses.

- [Azariah son of Amaziah king of Judah began to reign. He was sixteen years old when he became king, and he reigned in Jerusalem fifty-two years. His mother's name was Jecoliah; she was from Jerusalem]

- [Uzziah, who was sixteen years old, and made him king in place of his father Amaziah. - Uzziah was sixteen years old when he became king, and he reigned in Jerusalem fifty-two years. His mother's name was Jecoliah; she was from Jerusalem]

{**Important note...** There are two great deceptions revealed in both descriptions. For example: The following two descriptions **(and he reigned in Jerusalem fifty-two years. His mother's name was Jecoliah; she was from Jerusalem)** and **(and he reigned in Jerusalem fifty-two years. His mother's name was Jecoliah; she was from Jerusalem)** are both written deceptively and represent another trap. As explained previously, the Kingdom of Jerusalem will not emerge until after the second exodus period (as representing the fall of the Ram Age). Thus, the city called Jerusalem, the Holy City, will not emerge until the bronze Age]}

(Note26: The next deception is revealed by the following. One of the following two names, Azariah and Uzziah does not represent a king of Judah but represents a Chief priest. Within the descriptions of 2nd Chronicle 26:19-20, reveals a major clue as to which of them belongs to the priestly division of Aaron (representing a descendant of Aaron), and which of them does not!))

Look closely at the bold portion in the description of 2nd Chronicles 26:19-20 below,

[**Uzziah, who had a censer in his hand ready to burn incense, became angry**. While he was raging at the priests in their presence before the incense altar in the Lord's temple, leprosy broke out on his forehead. **When Azariah the Chief priest and all the other priests looked at him,** they saw that he had leprosy on his forehead, so they hurried him out]

(Note27: Azariah the Chief priest represents a descendant of Aaron and belongs to the priestly division of Aaron (does not represent a king of Judah). Thus, the titled description 'Chief priest, High priest, or Levite' is symbolic for representing an 'elder of Judah' (also known as a descendant of Aaron). This revelation corresponds to the following descriptions 'But only you and your sons may serve as priests in connection with everything at the altar and inside the curtain. I am giving you the service of the priesthood as a gift. Anyone else who comes near the sanctuary is to be put to death' – Numbers 18:7, as well as the following description '"Aaron's sacred garments will belong to his descendants so that they can be anointed and ordained in them' – 1st Chronicles 23:28. Therefore, only king Uzziah represents a king of Judah and does not represent a descendant of Aaron (succeeded his father Amaziah as King of Judah))

Here is the next clue: The following description **'Those who grieve and lament'** corresponds to the **priestly division of Aaron** and represents the name of the following house: [The House of Judah].

(Note28: The House of Judah (priestly division of Aaron), represents the Most Holy Place in the ancient city of Megiddo, also known as the Temple of the Lord. Thus, only a descendant of Aaron can enter the Temple of the Lord. This revelation corresponds to the following description 'He answered, "Haven't you read what David did when he and his companions were hungry? He entered the house of God, and he and his companions ate the consecrated bread—which was not lawful for them to do, but only for the priests' – Matthew 12:3-4)

(Note29: There is a great revelation revealed concerning why the House of Judah (descendants of Aaron), grieve and lament. This revelation will be revealed behind the understanding of the following description **'over all the detestable things that are done in it.'** *To start, you must look closely at the description of 2nd Kings 18:4)*

Look closely at the following description of 2nd Kings 18:4 below,

[He removed the high places, smashed the sacred stones and cut down the Asherah poles. He broke into pieces the bronze snake Moses had made, for up to that time the Israelites had been burning incense to it. (It was called Nehushtan.)]

(Note30: There are two major clues revealed by this description. To understand the 1st clue, you must first understand the symbolic meaning of what the Asherah poles represent)

To understand the mystery of the Asherah poles look closely at the bold portion in the following description of Exodus 7:9 below,

['When Pharaoh says to you, 'perform a miracle,' **then say to Aaron, "Take your staff and throw it down before Pharaoh,' and it will become a snake."**]

(Note31: The **Asherah pole** *is symbolic and corresponds to the following description* **'the bronze snake Moses had made'** *(also called the Nehushtan))*

Here is the next clue: The **Asherah pole** corresponds to the **bronze snake** *(called the Neheshtan)* and represents the following staff: [Aaron's wooden staff].

(Note32: The following description **'He broke into pieces the bronze snake Moses had made'** *is incorrect! For example: Moses did not make the bronze snake for reasons the bronze snake represents Aaron's wooden staff. This revelation corresponds to the following description* **'then say to Aaron, "Take your staff and throw it down before Pharaoh, and it will become a snake'** *- Exodus 7:9. Thus, the color of Aaron's wooden staff (brownish appearance) corresponds to the color of the Nehushtan (bronze snake). This revelation reveals the meaning behind the following description 'The LORD said to Moses, "Put back Aaron's staff in front of the ark of the covenant law, to be kept as a sign to the rebellious' - Numbers 17:10)*

*(Note33: The next major clue is to understand the symbolic meaning of what the **'High Places'** represent. This clue can be found in the description of Deuteronomy 34:5-6)*

Look closely at the bold portion of the following description of Deuteronomy 34:5-6 below,

[And Moses the servant of the Lord died there in Moab, as the Lord had said. **He buried him in Moab, in the valley opposite Beth Peor, but to this day no one knows where his grave is**]

*(Note34: The 'High Place' is symbolic and corresponds to the very place where Moses died and was buried (Mount Nebo). Mount Nebo is also symbolic and corresponds to the High Mountain, also referred to as the Mountain of God. In the region where this mountain resides is also called the mountain of Esau also referred to as Mount Ebal, also called the sacred mountain or the Mountain of the Lord.' The **High Place** corresponds to the description in the verse of Ezekiel 39:11 – 'It will block the way of travelers, because Gog and all his hordes will be buried there. So, it will be called the Valley of Hamon Gog.' This description **'It will block the way of travelers'** corresponds to the description in the verse of Ezekiel 41:11 – **'and the base adjoining the open area was five cubits wide all around'**. The 'base adjoining the open area' is also symbolic and corresponds to the bold description – 'The king asked, **"What is that tombstone I see?"** The people of the city said, "It marks the tomb of the man of God who came from Judah' – 2nd Kings 23:17., Thus, representing a tombstone shaped mountain. This revelation will be revealed in more detail in the 2nd and 3rd Chronicles of the Elijah Doctrine)*

Here is the next clue: The **High Place** *(sacred mountain)* corresponds to the **Base adjoining the open area** and represents the following place: [The Foot of the Mountain *(also known as the tombstone shaped mountain)*]!

*(Note35: Mount Nebo as previously revealed is symbolic and corresponds to the High Mountain in the land of Judah, also known as the sacred mountain, or the Mountain of the Lord (Holy Mountain), also called the Mountain of God. This revelation corresponds to the following description 'You will bring them in and plant them on the mountain of your inheritance- the place, LORD, you made for your dwelling, the sanctuary, Lord, your hands established' – Exodus 15:17. The **High Place**, however, represent the **Foot of the mountain** also known as the **Most Holy Place**. This area will also be revealed in more detail in the 2nd and 3rd Chronicles of the Elijah Doctrine)*

Here is the next [vital clue]: The following description **'over all the detestable things that are done in it'** corresponds to the following detestable act that were done in the city of Megiddo: [The elders of Judah grieved over Moses ***(by longing for Moses at the Foot of the Mountain (High Place)***] - And - [The elders of Judah lament over Moses ***(by burning incense to Aaron's wooden staff (Asherah pole)***].

*(Note36: When the House of Judah (priestly division of Aaron) grieved over Moses, they did so in front of the tombstone shaped mountain, known as the Foot of the mountain. And when the House of Judah (priestly division of Aaron) lamented Moses, they did so, by crying out in longing for Moses, while burning incense to Aaron's wooden staff. Though it was Moses who led the Israelites through the wilderness and established the Mosaic Law (maintained by the House of Judah), it was the longing of Moses that became the detestable act that was committed by the House of Judah, in the ancient city called Megiddo, (the city where I chose to put my name). This revelation reveals the meaning behind the following description **"But do not think I will accuse you before the Father. Your accuser is Moses, on whom your hopes are set'** – John 5:45.)*

Here is the final clue: The House of Judah **grieved** over the high place, known as the tombstone shaped mountain, over Moses, by longing for his return at the Foot of the Mountain...

...And the House of Judah **lament** over Moses, by crying out to him, while burning incense to Aaron's wooden staff, the Asherah pole, called the Nehushtan...

The next thing you must do is look closely at the bold portion in the following description of Ezekiel 9:5.

> [As I listened, **he said to the others, "Follow him through the city and kill without showing pity or compassion**]

(Note37: This description reveals two major clues. The first clue is revealed behind the number 144,000. Within this number will reveal which of the two nations (Ephraim or Judah), in which the five living creatures (representing five apocalyptic riders) are being sent to kill without showing pity or compassion))

Look closely at the following description of Revelation 7:4 below,

[Then I heard the number of those who were sealed: 144,000 from all the tribes of Israel]

(Note38: This verse is structurally written deceptively. The number 144,000 is symbolic and does not represent the number of those sealed. One of the reasons is due to Judah not representing a tribe. Thus, by removing Judah from the description the math 12,000 x 11, does not total 144,000 (12,000 x 11 = 132,000), as it would if you multiplied 12,000 x 12 (12 x 12 = 144,000). This means a tribe is missing from the equation. To identify the true number, you must locate a hidden clue revealed in the descriptions of Revelation 7:5-8))

Remove the tribe of Judah and look closely at the following descriptions of Revelation 7:5-8 as seen below,

12- [From the tribes of *Reuben* 12,000 were sealed]
13- [From the tribes of *Gad* 12,000 were sealed]
14- [From the tribes of *Asher* 12,000 were sealed]
15- [From the tribes of *Naphtali* 12,000 were sealed]
16- [From the tribes of *Manasseh* 12,000 were sealed]
17- [From the tribe of *Simeon* 12,000 were sealed]
18- [From the tribe of *Levi* 12,000 were sealed]
19- [From the tribe of *Issachar* 12,000 were sealed]
20- [From the tribe of *Zebulon* 12,000 were sealed]
21- [From the tribe of *Joseph* 12,000 were sealed]
22- [From the tribe of *Benjamin* 12,000 were sealed]

(Note39: To identify the true number of those sealed you must use division to calculate the true sum. For example: If you add these [ten tribes] with the [single tribe] you will conclude the total number of the tribes))

Here is the [1st clue]: The true number of tribes represents the following number: [Eleven].

{**Important note... The true number of those sealed does not correspond to the 12 tribes of Israel (thus, dividing 12,000/144,000 = 12) but represents the number Eleven.** This revelation corresponds to the following description 'I will take the kingdom from his son's hands and give you ten tribes. I will give one tribe to his son so that David my servant may always have a lamp before me' – 1st Kings 11:34-36 (thus, reflecting eleven tribes total). The eleven tribes collectively seal the 4th Kingdom of Clay, known as the City of David. As revealed previously, the tribe of Judah does not represent a tribe because the tribe of Benjamin emerges into the Nation of Judah}

(Note40: The second clue is revealed by dividing the 4th kingdom (The City of David), into two nations to reflect a divided kingdom by dividing the eleven tribes to reflect their respective nations)

Next, use the base decoder regarding the (ten horns) and (beast) to reflect a divided kingdom as seen below,

- {Ten Horns} = [Ten kings = Ten tribes = *I will take the kingdom from his son's hands and give you ten tribes* = **Tribes of Ephraim, Manasseh, Naphtali, Dan, Asher, Issachar, Zebulon, Simeon, Reuben, and Gad** = Jeroboam king of Ephraim = **Nation of Ephraim (land of Israel)** = *who are yet to receive a kingdom of their own* = Kingdom of Samaria *(descendants of Esau)*]

- {Beast} = [**single tribe** = *I will give one tribe to his son* = **Tribe of Benjamin** = *remained in the city* = **Nation of Judah** = Rehoboam king of Judah = Kingdom of Jerusalem *(descendants of Jacob)*]

(Note41: Within one of these two nations reveals the name of the city where the five apocalyptic riders have been sent to destroy)

Here is the 2nd clue: The name of the city *(where five apocalyptic riders have been sent)* corresponds to the following city that resides in the Land of Judah: [The ancient city called Megiddo]!

The next thing you must do is look closely at the bold portion in the following description of Ezekiel 9:6.

[Slaughter old men, young men and maidens, women and children, but do not touch anyone who has the mark. **Begin at my sanctuary." So they began with the elders who were in front of the temple**]

(Note42: Within this description reveals two major clues. The first clue is revealed behind the words 'my sanctuary.' For example: The sanctuary represents the Most Holy Place in the ancient city of Megiddo (the city where I chose to put my name - 1st Kings 11:36))

Here is the next clue: The **sanctuary** corresponds to the **Most Holy Place** and represents the following house in the ancient city of Megiddo: [The house of God].

(Note43: The second clue is revealed behind the following description 'So they began with the elders who were in front of the temple'. To reveal this clue, you must first locate another clue hidden in the description of Revelation 1:20)

Look closely at the following description of Revelation 1:20 below,

[The mystery of the seven stars that you saw in my right hand and of the seven golden lampstands is this: **The seven stars are the angels of the seven churches**, and the seven lampstands are the seven churches]

*(Note44: This verse is written deceptively and reveals a hidden clue: For example: You must merge the **'seven lampstands'** with the description of Revelation 17:9. For example: The **golden lampstands** correspond to **seven horns** that are **seven heads and seven hills**, on which the woman sits. Thus, the seven golden lampstands represent **seven kings**.)*

The next revealing clue is found in the book of Revelation 1:4,

[To the seven churches in the province of Asia: Grace and peace to you from him who is, and who was, and who is to come, **and from the seven spirits before his throne**]

Next, remove the bold portion from both descriptions and merge them together as seen below,

[seven stars = seven spirits]

Here, you will discover the paradox of how the **seven stars** that are the angels of the seven churches, is also symbolic and correspond to the **seven spirits** before the throne.

{Important note… The following description **'from him who is, and who was, and who is to come'** is also symbolic and corresponds to the description **'and among the lampstands was someone like a son of man'**. Thus, it corresponds to the 'solid gold lampstand' as representing the woman as the '8th king'}

The next thing you must do is bring back the base decoder and merge the revelations together into the correct places as seen below,

{Two horns (*ram*)} = [two heads = two hills = two kings] = **[two stars = Two spirits before his throne** = 1st and 2nd men = two golden lampstands]

{Larger horn (*goat*)} = [third head = third hill = 3RD king] = [3rd **star = 3rd spirit before his throne** = 3rd man = 3rd golden lampstand]

{1ST prominent horn} = [4TH head = 4TH hill = 4TH king] = [4th **star = 4th spirit before his throne** = 4th man = 4th golden lampstand]

{2ND prominent horn} = [5TH head = 5TH hill = 5TH king] = [5th **star = 5th spirit before his throne** = 5th man = 5th golden lampstand]

{3RD prominent horn} = [6TH head = 6TH hill = 6TH king] = [6th **star = 6th spirit before his throne** = 6th man = 6th golden lampstand]

{4TH prominent horn} = [7TH head = 7TH hill = 7TH king] = [7th **star = 7th spirit before his throne** = 7th man = 7th golden lampstand] = [Satan]

Next, look closely at the description in the verse of 1ST Chronicles 15:24.

[Shebaniah, Joshaphat, Nethanel, Amasai, Zechariah, Benaiah and Eliezer the priests were to blow trumpets before the ark of God]

Here, you will discover that the seven spirits before the throne is symbolic and corresponds to the seven priests blowing their trumpets before the ark of God, as representing seven elders of Judah.

Here is the 2nd clue: The **elders in front of the temple** correspond to **seven stars**, that are **seven angels of the seven churches**, as corresponding to '**seven spirits before his throne** and represents **seven angels blasting seven trumpets** as **seven priests blowing their trumpets before the altar**.

The next thing you must do is bring back the base decoder and merge the revelations together into the correct places as seen below,

{Two horns (*ram*)} = [two heads = two hills = two kings] = [two stars = Two spirits before his throne = **1ˢᵗ and 2ⁿᵈ angels blasting two trumpets**] = [**1ˢᵗ and 2ⁿᵈ priests** *(blowing trumpets)* = 1ˢᵗ and 2ⁿᵈ men = **1ˢᵗ and 2ⁿᵈ elders of Judah** = two golden lampstands]

{Larger horn (*goat*)} = [third head = third hill = 3ᴿᴰ king] = [3ʳᵈ star = 3ʳᵈ spirit before his throne = **3ʳᵈ angel blasting 3ʳᵈ trumpet**] = [**3ʳᵈ priest** *(blowing trumpet)* = 3ʳᵈ man = **3ʳᵈ elder of Judah** = 3ʳᵈ golden lampstand]

{1ˢᵀ prominent horn} = [4ᵀᴴ head = 4ᵀᴴ hill = 4ᵀᴴ king] = [4ᵗʰ star = 4ᵗʰ spirit before his throne = **4ᵗʰ angel blasting 4ᵗʰ trumpet**] = [**4ᵗʰ priest** *(blowing trumpet)* = 4ᵗʰ man = **4ᵗʰ elder of Judah** = 4ᵗʰ golden lampstand]

{2ᴺᴰ prominent horn} = [5ᵀᴴ head = 5ᵀᴴ hill = 5ᵀᴴ king] = [5ᵗʰ star = 5ᵗʰ spirit before his throne = **5ᵗʰ angel blasting 5ᵗʰ trumpet**] = [**5ᵗʰ priest** *(blowing trumpet)* = 5ᵗʰ man = **5ᵗʰ elder of Judah** = 5ᵗʰ golden lampstand]

{3ᴿᴰ prominent horn} = [6ᵀᴴ head = 6ᵀᴴ hill = 6ᵀᴴ king] = [6ᵗʰ star = 6ᵗʰ spirit before his throne = **6ᵗʰ angel blasting 7ᵗʰ trumpet**] = [**6ᵗʰ priest** *(blowing trumpet)* = 6ᵗʰ man = **6ᵗʰ elder of Judah** = 6ᵗʰ golden lampstand]

{4ᵀᴴ prominent horn} = [7ᵀᴴ head = 7ᵀᴴ hill = 7ᵀᴴ king] = [7ᵗʰ star = 7ᵗʰ spirit before his throne = **7ᵗʰ angel blasting 7ᵗʰ trumpet**] = [**7ᵗʰ priest** *(blowing trumpet)* = 7ᵗʰ man = **7ᵗʰ elder of Judah** = 7ᵗʰ golden lampstand] = [Satan]

(Note45: The seven trumpets also reveal another major clue. For example: The seven trumpets correspond to seven types of sounds. To reveal this clue, you must look closely the following description of 1ˢᵀ Chronicles 15:28)

Look closely at the bold portion in the following description of 1ST Chronicles 15:28 below,

[So all Israel brought up the ark of the covenant of the Lord with shouts, with the sounding of rams,' horns and trumpets, and of cymbals, and the playing of Lyres and Harps]

*(Note46: To reveal this clue, you must also merge the seven types of sounds with the description of Revelation 17:9. For example: The **seven types of sounds** correspond to **seven horns** that are **seven heads and seven hills**, on which the woman sits. Thus, the 'seven sounds' also represents **seven kings**.)*

Here is the next clue: The **seven trumpets** correspond to the following sounds: [shouts, sounding of rams, horns, trumpets, cymbals, Lyres and Harps].

The next thing you must do is bring back the base decoder and merge the revelations together into the correct places as seen below,

{Two horns *(ram)*} = [two heads = two hills = two kings] = [two stars = 1st and 2nd angels blasting two trumpets] = [1st and 2nd priests *(blowing trumpets)* = **horns and sounding of rams** = 1st and 2nd men = 1st and 2nd elders of Judah = two golden lampstands]

{Larger horn *(goat)*} = [third head = third hill = 3RD king] = [3rd star = 3rd angel blasting 3rd trumpet] = [3rd priest *(blowing trumpet)* = **trumpets** = 3rd man = 3rd elder of Judah = 3rd golden lampstand]

{1ST prominent horn} = [4TH head = 4TH hill = 4TH king] = [4th star = 4th angel blasting 4th trumpet] = [4th priest *(blowing trumpet)* = **Harps** = 4th man = 4th elder of Judah = 4th golden lampstand]

{2ND prominent horn} = [5TH head = 5TH hill = 5TH king] = [5th star = 5th angel blasting 5th trumpet] = [5th priest *(blowing trumpet)* = **cymbals** = 5th man = 5th elder of Judah = 5th golden lampstand]

{3RD prominent horn} = [6TH head = 6TH hill = 6TH king] = [6th star = 6th angel blasting 6th trumpet] = [6th priest *(blowing trumpet)* = **Lyres** = 6th man = 6th elder of Judah = 6th golden lampstand]

{4TH prominent horn} = [7TH head = 7TH hill = 7TH king] = [7th star = 7th angel blasting 7th trumpet] = [7th priest *(blowing trumpet)* = **shouts** = 7th man = 7th elder of Judah = 7th golden lampstand] = [Satan]

(Note47: The seven types of sounds also reveal another major clue. To reveal this clue, you must look closely at the following description of 1ST Chronicles 6:31)

Look closely at the bold portion in the following description of 1ST Chronicles 6:31 below,

[These are the men David put in charge of the **music in the house of the Lord** after the ark came to rest there]

(Note48: The seven types of sounds correspond to the description of 1st Chronicles (music in the house of the Lord) and represents music in the Temple of the Lord)

Here is the next [vital clue]: The **seven types of sounds *(shouts, sounding of rams, horns, trumpets, cymbals, Lyres and Harps)*** correspond to '**Music in the house of the Lord'** *(temple of the Lord)* and represent sounds from the following house: [The House of Judah].

(Note49: The five apocalyptic riders (as representing five living creatures) have been sent to the ancient city called Megiddo, to destroy the House of Judah!)

The next thing you must do is look closely at the following description of Ezekiel 9:7.

[Defile the temple and fill the courts with the slain. Go!]

(Note50: This description reveals another major clue. For example: The temple of the Lord (Most Holy Place) corresponds to the House of Judah (priestly division of Aaron). Thus, the clue is revealed in description of 2nd Chronicles 36:19)

Look closely at the bold portion in the following description of 2nd Chronicles below,

[**They set fire to God's temple and broke down the wall of Jerusalem**; they burned all the palaces and destroyed everything of value there]

(Note51: This description is written deceptively. For example. The wall of Jerusalem does not reside in the land of Judah because Jerusalem does not emerge until after the 2nd exodus. Therefore, the wall of Jerusalem is symbolic and corresponds to the wall of Megiddo. The burning of the temple of God (Temple of the Lord) takes place in the city called Megiddo. This ancient city will become known as the ruined city of Megiddo (besieged by the Babylonian Empire). This revelation reveals the meaning behind the bold portion of this description **'But exclude the courtyard outside the temple. Do not measure it, because it has been given over to the nations, and they will trample the holy city** *for forty-two months – Revelation 11:2.')*

(Note52: This revelation also corresponds to the following description **'He carried to Babylon all the articles from the temple of God, both large and small, and the treasures of the LORD's temple and the treasures of the king and his officials'** *– 2nd Chronicles 36:18)*

Here is the next clue" The **Defiling of the temple** corresponds to the description **'fill the courts with the slain'** and represents the following revelation: [The burning of the Temple of the Lord]!

The next thing you must do is look closely at the following description of Ezekiel 9:9-10.

> [The sin of the house of Israel and Judah is exceedingly great; the land is full of bloodshed and the city is full of injustice. So I will not look on them with pity or spare them, but I will bring down on their own heads what they have done."]

(Note53: This description is also written deceptively. For example. The house of Israel corresponds to the nation of Ephraim (the land of Israel), also known as the Kingdom of Samaria. And the House of Judah corresponds to the land of Judah, also known as the Nation of Judah. If you recall from the verse of Isaiah, **'Ephraim** *(the House of Israel)* **broke away from Judah'** *(the House of Judah) - Isaiah 7:17))*

Here is the next clue: The following description **'The sin of the house of Judah is exceedingly great'** corresponds to the **'burning of the Temple of the Lord'** as well as the **'destroyed city of Megiddo'** *(the land is full of bloodshed and the city is full of injustice)* and represents the following revelation regarding the Nation of Judah: [The land of Judah has fallen by the rise of the Babylonian Empire]!

The final thing you must do is look closely at the following description of Ezekiel 9:11.

> [Then the man in linen with the writing kit at his side brought back word, saying, "I have done as you commanded]

(Note54: This description reveals another major clue. For example: Within the mystery of this description will reveal the meaning behind the following title: **'Lord of Lords.'** *To start, you must locate another hidden clue revealed in the description of Daniel 8:13.)*

Look closely the description of Daniel 8:13 below,

> [the rebellion that causes desolation, and the surrender of the sanctuary and of the host that will be trampled underfoot]

*(Note55: The surrender of the sanctuary represents the burning of the Temple of the Lord. The **host** is symbolic and corresponds to one of the four apocalyptic riders. Thus, the host that will be trampled underfoot corresponds to the fall of Satan, the 7th king. Therefore, the 5th prominent horn representing an 8th king, has trampled down the 4th prominent horn as representing the 7th king. This revelation also reveals another paradox. For example, the host of heaven (heavenly realm) corresponds to the lord of the sanctuary (earthly realm))*

Here is the [1st vital clue]: The following description **'I have done as you commanded'** corresponds to the **'fall of Satan's sanctuary'** (Temple of the Lord) and reveals the **'5th apocalyptic rider'** as representing the **'woman'** (Someone like a son of man) as the **'8th king'** to represent the following title bestowed upon her: [Lord of Lords]!

*(Note56: This revelation reveals the meaning behind the bolded portions of the following verse, **'I know where you live--where Satan has his throne.** Yet you remain true to my name. You did not renounce your faith in me, not even in the days of Antipas, my faithful witness, **who was put to death in your city where Satan lives'** – Revelation 2:13)*

*(Note57: This description 'I know where you live' is symbolic and corresponds to the Land of Judah. The next part of the description '--where Satan has his throne' is also symbolic and corresponds to the Temple of the Lord. And this part of the description 'in your city where Satan lives' is symbolic and corresponds to the city called Megiddo. This revelation reveals the meaning behind this description **'But it was Solomon who built a house for him. "However, the Most High does not live in houses made by human hands. As the prophet says: "'Heaven is my throne, and the earth is my footstool. What kind of house will you build for me? Or where will my resting place be?'** – Acts 7:47-49. This revelation reveals another deception. For example. The following description **'the city where I chose to put my name'** is incorrect! This city does not represent the true city where the God of David chose to put his name. In fact, the city never truly existed! Here lies the real deception. The city of Megiddo, which resides within the Land of Judah, represents the true city where Satan, the host of heaven, and Lord over the Temple of the Lord (The*

House of God), chose to put his name! This revelation reveals the meaning behind the following description **'And the LORD said to Satan, "Where have you come from?" Satan answered the LORD, "From roaming throughout the earth, going back and forth on it." – Job 2:2)**

(Note58: This description 'I have done as you commanded' as representing the fall of Satan's sanctuary, the House of God as well as the fall of Satan's city, the city of Megiddo, also reveals the meaning behind this description 'It grew until it reached the host of the heavens, and it threw some of the starry host down to the earth and trampled on them' – Daniel 8:10. For example, this part of the description **'It grew until it reached the host of the heavens'**, *represents the rise of the 5th prominent horn that is a 5th beast as representing the 5th living creature as the 5th apocalyptic rider. And this part of the description* **'and it threw some of the starry host down to the earth and trampled on them'** *represents the four apocalyptic riders that were cast down from the heavenly realm upon the earth by the 5th apocalyptic rider. The place where they were trampled upon represents the city called Megiddo. Thus, the 4th prominent horn that is the 4th beast as representing the 4th living creature as the 4th apocalyptic rider, represents the* **host of heaven** *(as representing Satan the mighty angel) and the* **Lord of the sanctuary** *(as representing the House of God). This revelation also reveals the meaning behind the description* **"From roaming throughout the earth, going back and forth on it." – Job 2:2))**

And behold, she who was considered unformidable by the seven men as representing seven kings as seven angels standing before the Ancient of Days, now has this title bestowed upon her, **Lord of Lords**, for she has trample down Satan, the mighty 7th king, who represents the mighty angel as the host of the heavens, and the Lord of the sanctuary, that is the Temple of the Lord, known also as the House of God.

The next thing you must do is bring back the base decoder regarding the 5th prominent horn and merge the revelations together into the correct place as seen below,

- [5th prominent horn] = [Solid gold lampstand = Someone like a son of man = Man clothed in linen (writing kit at his side) = *He came and took the scroll from the right hand of him who sat on the throne! = The armies of heaven were following him, riding on white horses and dressed in fine linen, white and clean = (And from His mouth proceeds a sharp sword)* = 8th king = King of Kings = **Lord of Lords** = Naphtali] = [5th beast = Woman = 5th living creature = Lamb looking as if slain *(will hate the prostitute)* = 5th cherubim = 5th chariot = 5th spirit = 5th angel = 5th guard of the city = 5th apocalyptic rider *(from His mouth proceeds a sharp sword)* = A great hailstorm]

(Note59: The fall of Satan's sanctuary (where Satan has his throne), and the city of Megiddo (city were Satan lives), reveals the fall of the Nation of Judah (besieged by the Empire of Babylon). The fall of the Nation of Judah reveals the meaning behind the following description - **"On that day, I will banish the names of the idols from the land, and they will be remembered no more," declares the LORD Almighty. "I will remove both the prophets and the spirit of impurity from the land. And if anyone still prophesies, their father and mother, to whom they were born, will say to them, 'You must die, because you have told lies in the LORD's name. Then their own parents will stab the one who prophesies'** *– Zechariah 13:2-3.)*

(Note60: The fall of the Nation of Judah also reveals the meaning behind the 2nd side of the flying cursed scroll as revealed in the bold part of the description in the verse of Zechariah 5:3 - "This is the curse that is going out over the whole land; for according to what it says on one side, every thief will be banished, **and according to what it says on the other, everyone who swears falsely will be banished***)*

THE FALL OF THE KINGDOM OF SAMARIA (The land of Israel)

The first thing you must do is look closely at the bold portion in the following description of Revelation 10:14.

[The sixth angel, who has the trumpet, is told to **release the four angels who are bound at the great river Euphrates**]

(Note61: There is a hidden clue revealed in this description. For example: The four angels (bound at the great river Euphrates) correspond to four chariots horses positioned in the sky (as representing four guards of the city))

The next thing you must do is look closely at the following description of Zechariah 6:5.

[These are the four spirits of heaven, going out from standing in the presence of the Lord]

*(Note62: Within this description reveals another hidden clue. For example: The **four angels** correspond to **four spirits of heaven** and represent **four chariot horses** (positioned in the sky). The clue is revealed in the description of Zechariah 6:7)*

Look closely at the following description of the Zechariah 6:7 below,

[When the powerful horses went out, they were straining to go throughout the earth. And he said, "Go throughout the earth!" So they went throughout the earth]

*(Note63: This description '**Go throughout the earth! So they went throughout the earth**' correspond to the four spirits of heaven as representing the four powerful horses, and correspond to the following description '**The one with the black horses is going toward the north country, the one with the white horses toward the west, and the one with the dappled horses toward the south**' – Zechariah 6:6. Thus, the red horses remained in the east!)*

(Note64: There is also another hidden clue revealed in the description of Zechariah 6:7. For example: The following four directions where the horses are going (north, west, south and east), is symbolic and corresponds to four directions in the sky. The clue is revealed in the description of Revelation 7:1))

Look closely at the description of Revelation 7:1 below,

> [After this I saw four angels standing at the four corners of the earth, holding back the four winds of the earth]

(Note65: The four directions, north, west, south and east, correspond to four corners of the earth)

Here is the next clue: The **four winds of heaven** correspond to **four angels standing at the four corners of the earth** as representing **four directions (north, west, south and east)** and represent the following revelation: [Four winds of the earth].

The next thing you must do is bring back the base decoder regarding the four prominent horns and merge the revelations together in the correct places as seen below,

- {1ST prominent horn} = [4TH head = 4TH hill = 4TH king] = [4th star = 4th angel blasting 4th trumpet] = [4th priest *(blowing trumpet)* = Harps = 4th man = 4th elder of Judah = 4th golden lampstand] = [1ST beast = lion = 1ST living creature = = like a lion = 1ST cherubim = 1ST chariot = Brown horses = 1ST spirit = **North = 1st wind of the earth** = 1ST angel = 1ST guard of the city = 1ST apocalyptic rider *(Its rider held a bow)* = Brown horses = Peals of thunder] = [1ST kingdom]

- {2ND prominent horn} = [5TH head = 5TH hill = 5TH king] = [5th star = 5th angel blasting 5th trumpet] = [5th priest *(blowing trumpet)* = cymbals = 5th man = 5th elder of Judah = 5th golden lampstand] = [2ND beast = bear = 2ND living creature = = like an ox = 2ND cherubim = 2ND chariot = Black horses = 2ND spirit = **South = 2nd wind of the earth** = 2ND angel = 2ND guard of the city = 2ND apocalyptic rider *(Its rider was holding a pair of scales in his hand)* = Black horses = Rumblings] = [2ND kingdom]

- {3ᴿᴰ prominent horn} = [6ᵀᴴ head = 6ᵀᴴ hill = 6ᵀᴴ king] = [6ᵗʰ star = 6ᵗʰ angel blasting 6ᵗʰ trumpet] = [6ᵗʰ priest *(blowing trumpet)* = Lyres = 6ᵗʰ man = 6ᵗʰ elder of Judah = 6ᵗʰ golden lampstand] = [3ᴿᴰ beast = leopard = 3ᴿᴰ living creature = face like a man = 3ᴿᴰ cherubim = 3ᴿᴰ chariot = Pale horses = 3ᴿᴰ spirit = **West = 3ʳᵈ wind of the earth** = 3ᴿᴰ angel = 3ᴿᴰ guard of the city = 3ᴿᴰ apocalyptic rider *(to kill by sword, famine and plague)* = Pale horses = Flashes of lightning] = [3ᴿᴰ kingdom]

- [4ᵀᴴ prominent horn] = [7ᵀᴴ head = 7ᵀᴴ hill = 7ᵀᴴ king *(And he was given a great sword)*] = [7ᵗʰ star = 7ᵗʰ angel blasting 7ᵗʰ trumpet] = [7ᵗʰ priest *(blowing trumpet)* = shouts = 7ᵗʰ man = 7ᵗʰ elder of Judah = 7ᵗʰ golden lampstand] = [4ᵀᴴ beast *(The beast and the ten horns you saw)* Beast coming out of the sea *(ancient serpent)* = Scarlet beast *(devil)* = Red dragon *(Satan)*] = [Satan *(name of a man)* = Mighty angel *(coming up from the east)* = Who is worthy to break the seals and open the scroll? = 4ᵀᴴ living creature = like a flying eagle = 4ᵀᴴ cherubim = 4ᵀᴴ chariot = Fiery red horses = 4ᵀᴴ spirit = **East = 4ᵗʰ wind of the earth** = 4ᵀᴴ angel = 4ᵀᴴ guard of the city = 4ᵀᴴ apocalyptic rider *(To him was given a large sword)* = Fiery red horses = Earthquake] = [Then I saw the beast and the kings of the earth and their armies gathered together to make war against the rider on the horse and his army] = [4ᵗʰ kingdom]

*(Note66: The four angels that are bound at the great river Euphrates means they are bound in the land of Assyria. Thus, this description **'release the four angels'**, means they are leaving the Assyrian Empire. There is another hidden clue revealed in the description of Isaiah 18:1-2, as to which land's they are being sent to)*

Look closely at the bold portion in the following description of Isaiah 18:1-2 below,

> [Woe to the land of whirring wings along the rivers of Cush, which sends envoys by sea in papyrus boats over the water. **Go, swift messengers, to a people tall and smooth-skinned, to a people feared far and wide, an aggressive nation of strange speech, whose land is divided by rivers**]

*(Note67: There is a major clue revealed in this description. For example: The following description **'release the four angels bound at the great river Euphrates'** corresponding to the description **'Go throughout the earth! So they went throughout the earth'** also correspond to this description **'Go, swift messengers'**. The hidden clue is revealed by where they are being sent. The clue is revealed by the understanding of this description **'Woe to the land of whirring wings along the rivers of Cush'**)*

*(Note68: The **land of whirring wings** corresponds to a land divided by two rivers (as representing the Blue and White Nile Rivers). Thus, the people of the land (**tall and smooth-skinned, a people feared far and wide, an aggressive nation of strange speech**), represent a people known as the Kushite Empire (would later give rise to the Nubian Empire). This land, divided by rivers is in the present-day country of Africa, known as Sudan (near the great temple of Abu Simbel))*

*(Note69: The **whirring wings** are symbolic and correspond to the Egyptian goddess, known as Isis (twin sister of Nephthys), both of whom are often depicted with outstretched wings. The Egyptian goddess Isis would become worshiped in ancient Egypt and throughout the years she would also come to be worshiped by the Romans (Thus, she would also become known throughout the world as a Pagan goddess). The land of Egypt also corresponds to the Empire of Kush (thus, Egypt fell during the 24th dynasty to the rise of the Kushite Empire and was ruled in the 25th dynasty by a Kushite Pharaoh. In this dynasty, the land of Egypt would become known by the Bible as the Wadi of Egypt. This revelation corresponds to the following description **'Sennacherib received a report that Tirhakah, the Cushite king of Egypt was marching out to fight against him'** - 2nd Kings 19:9)*

Here is the next clue: The following description **'Release the four angels bound at the Euphrates River'** correspond to the description **'Go, swift messengers** *(to the land of whirring wings)*,' and represents the following land to which they have been sent: [The Wadi of Egypt *(also known as the Kushite Empire)*]!

The next thing you must do is bring back the base decoder regarding the four prominent horns and merge the revelations together in the correct places as seen below,

- {1ST prominent horn} = [4TH head = 4TH hill = 4TH king] = [4th star = 4th angel blasting 4th trumpet] = [4th priest *(blowing trumpet)* = Harps = 4th man = 4th elder of Judah = 4th golden lampstand] = [1ST beast = lion = 1ST living creature = like a lion = 1ST cherubim = 1ST chariot = Brown horses = 1ST spirit = 1ST angel = **1ST swift messenger** = North = 1st wind of the earth = 1ST guard of the city = 1ST apocalyptic rider *(Its rider held a bow)* = Brown horses = Peals of thunder] = [1ST kingdom]

- {2ND prominent horn} = [5TH head = 5TH hill = 5TH king] = [5th star = 5th angel blasting 5th trumpet] = [5th priest *(blowing trumpet)* = cymbals = 5th man = 5th elder of Judah = 5th golden lampstand] = [2ND beast = bear = 2ND living creature = like an ox = 2ND cherubim = 2ND chariot = Black horses = 2ND spirit = 2nd angel = **2ND swift messenger** = South = 2nd wind of the earth = 2ND guard of the city = 2ND apocalyptic rider *(Its rider was holding a pair of scales in his hand)* = Black horses = Rumblings] = [2ND kingdom]

- {3RD prominent horn} = [6TH head = 6TH hill = 6TH king] = [6th star = 6th angel blasting 6th trumpet] = [6th priest *(blowing trumpet)* = Lyres = 6th man = 6th elder of Judah = 6th golden lampstand] = [3RD beast = leopard = 3RD living creature = face like a man = 3RD cherubim = 3RD chariot = Pale horses = 3RD spirit = 3RD angel = **3RD swift messenger** = West = 3rd wind of the earth = 3RD guard of the city = 3RD apocalyptic rider *(to kill by sword, famine and plague)* = Pale horses = Flashes of lightning] = [3RD kingdom]

- [4TH prominent horn] = [7TH head = 7TH hill = 7TH king *(And he was given a great sword)*] = [7th star = 7th angel blasting 7th trumpet] = [7th priest *(blowing trumpet)* = shouts = 7th man = 7th elder of Judah = 7th golden lampstand] = [4TH beast *(The beast and the ten horns you saw)* = Beast coming out of the sea *(ancient serpent)* = Scarlet beast *(devil)* = Red dragon *(Satan)*] = [Satan *(name of a man)* = Mighty angel *(coming up from the east)* = Who is worthy to break the seals and open the scroll?= 4TH living creature = like a flying eagle = 4TH cherubim = 4TH chariot = Fiery red horses = 4TH spirit = East = 4th wind of the earth = 4TH angel = **4TH swift messenger** = 4TH guard of the city = 4TH apocalyptic rider *(To him was given a large sword)* =

Fiery red horses = Earthquake] = [Then I saw the beast and the kings of the earth and their armies gathered together to make war against the rider on the horse and his army] = [4ᵗʰ kingdom]

Next, place the following revelations regarding the Wadi of Egypt in the correct places as seen below,

- **{Empire of Kush} = [Invaded the land of Egypt *(Egypt fell in the 25ᵗʰ dynasty)*] = [Ancient Nubia** *(land of the Kushites)***] = [Land divided by rivers:** *(Blue Nile River)* **and** *(White Nile River)***] = [a people tall and smooth-skinned, to a people feared far and wide, an aggressive nation of strange speech]**

The next thing you must do is look closely at the bold portion in the description of Isaiah 18:1 below,

> [Woe to the land of whirring wings along the rivers of Cush, **which sends envoys by sea in papyrus boats over the water.** Go, swift messengers, to a people tall and smooth-skinned, to a people feared far and wide, an aggressive nation of strange speech, whose land is divided by rivers]

(Note70: This description reveals another clue. For example: The Empire of Kush (Wadi of Egypt) is sending envoys by sea in papyrus boats over the water to a foreign land. The name of this land reveals our next clue. The clue is revealed in the description of 2nd Kings 19:9)

Look closely at the following description of 2nd Kings 19:9 below,

> [Sennacherib received a report that *Tirhakah*, the *Cushite* king of Egypt was marching out to fight against him]

(Note71: The proper spelling of Cush or Cushite, is spelled with the letter "K", as representing Kush or Kushites. Thus, Pharaoh Tirhakah (Kushite Pharaoh of Egypt) will dispatch his envoys by sea over the waters of the Euphrates River))

Here is the next clue: Pharaoh Tirhakah *(Kushite Pharaoh of Egypt)* dispatches envoys by sea over the Euphrates River to the following land: [The Land of Assyria].

Next, place the following revelations regarding the land and king of Assyria in the correct places as seen below,

- {Pharaoh Tirhakah *(Pharoah of Egypt)*} = [Empire of Kush] = [Land divided by rivers: *(Blue Nile River)* and *(White Nile River)*] = [a people tall and smooth-skinned, to a people feared far and wide, an aggressive nation of strange speech] = [Invaded the land of Egypt *(Egypt fell in the 25th dynasty)*]

- {King Sennacherib *(Assyrian king)*} = [Assyrian Empire] = [Euphrates River]

Next, look closely at the bold portions in the following two descriptions below,

- 2nd Kings 17:5-6 - [**The king of Assyria invaded the entire land, marched against Samaria and laid siege** to it for three years. In the ninth year of Hoshea, the **king of Assyria captured Samaria and deported the Israelites to Assyria**]

- Isaiah 27:12 – [In that day **the Lord will thresh from the flowing Euphrates, to the Wadi of Egypt, and you, O Israelites, will be gathered up one by one. And in that day a great trumpet will sound. Those who were perishing in Assyria and those who were exiled in Egypt**]

*(Note72: There are two clues revealed in these descriptions. For example: **King Sennacherib** (King of Assyria) invaded the kingdom of Samaria and exiled the Samarian Israelites to the land of Assyria (2nd Kings 17:5-6). Example2: **Pharaoh Tirhakah** (Pharoah of Egypt) invaded the Assyrian Empire and defeated King Sennacherib, the King of Assyria (2nd Kings 19:9). This revelation reveals the meaning behind the bold part of the following description 'Isaiah said to them, "Tell your master, 'This is what the Lord says: Do not be afraid of what you have heard—those words with which the underlings of the king of Assyria have blasphemed me. Listen! **When he hears a certain report, I will make him want to return to his own country, and there I will have him cut down with the sword**' – Isaiah 37:6-7. Thus, the Assyrian Empire fell to the Kushite Empire)*

Here is the next clue: The kingdom of Samaria *(descendants of Esau)* fell by the rise of the Assyrian king *(King Sennacherib)* and were exiled by Pharaoh Tirhakah *(Pharoah of Egypt)* to the following land: [Wadi of Egypt *(The Empire of Kush)*]!

*(Note73: This revelation reveals the fall of the Kingdom of Samaria. The fall of the Kingdom of Samaria also reveals the meaning behind the 1st side of the flying cursed scroll as revealed in the bold part of the description in the verse of Zechariah 5:3 - "This is the curse that is going out over the whole land; **for according to what it says on one side, every thief will be banished,** and according to what it says on the other, everyone who swears falsely will be banished)*

Next, place the following revelations regarding the land of Cush and Assyria in the correct places as seen below,

- {Pharaoh Tirhakah *(Pharoah of Egypt)*} = [Empire of Kush] = [Land divided by rivers: *(Blue Nile River)* and *(White Nile River)*] = [a people tall and smooth-skinned, to a people feared far and wide, an aggressive nation of strange speech] = [Invaded the land of Egypt *(Egypt fell in the 25th dynasty)*] = **[Invaded the land of Assyria *(captured the Samarian Israelites)*]**

- {King Sennacherib *(Assyrian king)*} = [Assyrian Empire] = [Euphrates River] = **[Invaded the land of Samaria *(Captured the Samarian Israelites)*]**

The next thing you must do is bring back the base decoder regarding the (ten horns) and (beast), and merge the revelations together regarding the fate of (Samaria and Judah) into the correct places as seen below,

- {Ten Horns} = [Ten kings = Ten tribes = *I will take the kingdom from his son's hands and give you ten tribes* = Tribes of Ephraim, Manasseh, Naphtali, Dan, Asher, Issachar, Zebulon, Simeon, Reuben, and Gad = Jeroboam king of Ephraim = Nation of Ephraim = *who are yet to receive a kingdom of their own* Kingdom of Samaria *(descendants of Esau)*] = **[Conquered by the Assyrian Empire = Exodus by the Kushite Empire *(Wadi of Egypt)*]**

- {Beast} = [single tribe = *I will give one tribe to his son* = Tribe of Benjamin = *remained in the city* = Nation of Judah = Rehoboam king of Judah] = **[Conquered by the Babylonian Empire = Exodus by the Persian Empire]** = [Kingdom of Jerusalem *(descendants of Jacob)*]

Next, bring back the base decoder regarding the nation of Isaac *(golden calves)* and merge the revelations together regarding the fate of (Isaac's descendants) into the correct places as seen below,

- [Short horn] = {Nation of Isaac} = [Father of the first two nations born out of the 1st kingdom] = [Descendent generation = *another generation grew up*] = [Golden Calves *(descendants of Isaac)*] = [{Nation of Ephraim = Kingdom of Samaria *(Conquered by the Assyrian Empire)*] = [Nation of Judah *(Conquered by Babylonian Empire)*}] = **[Exiled to the land of Babylon and Assyria] = [End of the Ram Age *(Ending Timeline marker)*]** = [{**Exodus by the Kushite Empire *(Samarian Israelites deported to the land, Wadi of Egypt)*] = [Exodus by the Persian Empire *(Judah returns to the land of the east from they were taken)*]** = [Kingdom of Jerusalem *(Judah moves to the land of the west to build a new Kingdom)*}]

*(Note74: The following revelations revealed by the fate of Samaria and Judah, exiled to the following lands (Assyria and Babylon) represents the fall of the Ram Age! Thus, the fall of the **Kingdom of Samaria** (exodus by the Kushite Empire), and the fall of the **Nation of Judah** (exodus by the Persian Empire) marks the 2nd exodus period. The **2nd exodus period** also corresponds to the **fall of the Assyrian Empire** and the **fall of the Babylonian Empire** (as representing the fall of the Age of Silver). Thus, during the rise of the bronze Age the Kushite Empire having exiled the Samarians to the Wadi of Egypt, will no longer be called the Kushite Empire, but will become known by the Samarians, as the rise of the Nubian Empire)*

(Note75: During the rise of the Persian king, known as King Cyrus the great, the descendants of Judah would find themselves free from captivity and return to the land from which they were taken. This revelation corresponds to the bold part of this description 'This is what the Lord Almighty, the God of Israel, says: **"When I bring them back from captivity, the people in the land of Judah and in its towns will once again use these words: 'The Lord bless you, you prosperous city, you sacred mountain.'** *– Jeremiah 31:23. The descendants of Judah would later move on to build the Kingdom of Jerusalem in the Age of bronze. Thus, the rise of the Nubian Empire and the rise of the Persian Empire ushers in the bronze Age! The revelation regarding the element of bronze (Age of bronze) will be revealed in more detail in the next chapter)*

Congratulations!!! You have successfully completed the 3rd Chapter by revealing the true identity behind the title: Lord of Lords!

CHAPTER FOUR - 1st PHASE OF THE CRYPTEX PUZZLE - REVELATION OF THE SIGN

In this chapter, a new kingdom will rise out of the ashes and begin to take its shape. From this small tribe will arise a new Kingdom that will grow in power towards the north, the south, the east, and the west. This kingdom will emerge from a descendant of Esau, from a woman, who has been overlooked by the Church since the birth of Christianity. The revelation of her name, will reveal one of the greatest deceptions of Christianity...

...For it is she, who will give birth to the great sign and its revelation will topple the pillars of Religion and reveal the greatest deception of the Ages...!

The next thing you must do is look closely at the bold portion in the following description of Daniel 2:44

> [In the time of those kings, the God of heaven will set up a kingdom that will never be destroyed, nor will it be left to another people. It will crush all those kingdoms and bring them to an end, but it will itself endure forever]

(Note: The revelation revealed by this kingdom will be revealed in great detail. To begin, you must start by returning to the verse of Daniel 7:2))

THE RISE OF THE 5TH KINGDOM

The first thing you must do is bring back the following description of Daniel 7:2

[Daniel said: "In my vision at night I looked, and there before me were the four winds of heaven churning up the great sea]

(Note2: The four winds of the earth correspond to the four winds of heaven churning up the great sea)

The next thing you must do is bring back the base decoder regarding the four prominent horns and merge the revelations together in the correct places as seen below,

- {1ST prominent horn} = [4TH head = 4TH hill = 4TH king] = [4th star = 4th spirit before his throne = 4th angel blasting 4th trumpet] = [4th priest *(blowing trumpet)* = Harps = 4th man = 4th elder of Judah = 4th golden lampstand] = [1ST beast = lion = 1ST living creature = like a lion = 1ST cherubim = 1ST chariot = Brown horses = 1ST spirit = 1ST angel = North = 1st wind of the earth = **1st wind of heaven** *(churning up the great sea)* = 1ST guard of the city = 1ST apocalyptic rider *(Its rider held a bow)* = Brown horses = 1ST swift messenger = Peals of thunder] = [1ST kingdom]

- {2ND prominent horn} = [5TH head = 5TH hill = 5TH king] = [5th star = 5th spirit before his throne = 5th angel blasting 5th trumpet] = [5th priest *(blowing trumpet)* = cymbals = 5th man = 5th elder of Judah = 5th golden lampstand] = [2ND beast = bear = 2ND living creature = like an ox = 2ND cherubim = 2ND chariot = Black horses = 2ND spirit = 2ND angel = South = 2nd wind of the earth = **2nd wind of heaven** *(churning up the great sea)* = 2ND guard of the city = 2ND apocalyptic rider *(Its rider was holding a pair of scales in his hand)* = Black horses = 2ND swift messenger = Rumblings] = [2ND kingdom]

- {3RD prominent horn} = [6TH head = 6TH hill = 6TH king] = [6th star = 6th spirit before his throne = 6th angel blasting 6th trumpet] = [6th priest *(blowing trumpet)* = Lyres = 6th man = 6th elder of Judah = 6th golden lampstand] = [3RD beast = leopard = 3RD living creature = face like a man =

3RD cherubim = 3RD chariot = Pale horses = 3RD spirit = 3RD angel = West = 3rd wind of the earth = **3rd wind of heaven** *(churning up the great sea)* = 3RD guard of the city = 3RD apocalyptic rider *(to kill by sword, famine and plague)* = Pale horses = 3RD swift messenger = Flashes of lightning] = [3RD kingdom]

- {4^TH prominent horn} = [7TH head = 7TH hill = 7TH king *(And he was given a great sword)*] = [7th star = 7th spirit before his throne = 7th angel blasting 7th trumpet] = [7th priest *(blowing trumpet)* = shouts = 7th man = 7th elder of Judah = 7th golden lampstand] = [4TH beast *(The beast and the ten horns you saw)* = Beast coming out of the sea *(ancient serpent)* = Scarlet beast *(devil)* = Red dragon *(Satan)*] = [Satan *(name of a man)* = Mighty angel *(coming up from the east)* = Who is worthy to break the seals and open the scroll? 4TH living creature = like a flying eagle = 4TH cherubim = 4TH chariot = Fiery red horses = 4TH spirit = 4TH angel = East = 4th wind of the earth = **4th wind of heaven** *(churning up the great sea)* = 4TH guard of the city = 4TH apocalyptic rider *(To him was given a large sword)* = Fiery red horses = 4TH swift messenger = Earthquake] = [Then I saw the beast and the kings of the earth and their armies gathered together to make war against the rider on the horse and his army] = [4th kingdom]

Here is the next question. What is the name of this great sea?

(To answer this question, you must locate a set of clues hidden in the verses of Daniel 11:42-43)

Next, look closely at the bold portion in the following description of Daniel 11:42-43 below,

[He will extend his power over many countries; Egypt will not escape. **He will gain control of the treasures of gold and silver and all the riches of Egypt, with the Libyans and Nubians in submission**]

(Note3: The Libyans and Nubians correspond to two ancient regions known as Punt and Put, which is also part of the Empire of Nubia. The **land of the Libyans** *corresponds to the western region of Egypt (also known as the region land of Punt), and the* **land of the Nubians** *corresponds to the eastern region of Egypt (also known as the region land of Put). Within one of these two region lands of Egypt reveals the clue to uncovering the identity of the great sea!)*

Here is the next clue: The **great sea** corresponds to the **eastern region of Egypt, known as the land of Nubians** (region land of Put) and represents the following sea located at the eastern region of Egypt: [The Red Sea]!

(Note4: The following ancient kingdoms: Ethiopia, Napata, and Meroe, are also nations and kingdoms that descend from the Empire of Kush (known as ancient Nubia). The following ancient regions known as Put and Punt, were established before the invasion of Greece! Thus, this following description 'with the Libyans and Nubians in submission' is not a true representation of two regions conquered by Greece, nor is Greece a true representation of having conquered the entire Empire of Nubia (also known as the Wadi of Egypt). Therefore, Alexander of Greece, only overtook the region land of Put (eastern region), known today as Cairo-Egypt (the city of Alexandria))

The next thing you must do is place the following revelations in the correct places as seen below,

- {Pharaoh Tirhakah *(Pharoah of Egypt)*} = [Empire of Kush] = [Land divided by rivers: *(Blue Nile River)* and *(White Nile River)*] = [a people tall and smooth-skinned, to a people feared far and wide, an aggressive nation of strange speech] = [Invaded the land of Egypt *(Egypt fell in the 25th dynasty)*] = [Invaded the land of Assyria *(captured the Samarian Israelites)*] = **[Ancient Nubia *(land of the Kushites)*]** = **[Western region of upper Egypt = Punt *(Libyans)*]** and **[Eastern region of upper Egypt = Put *(Nubians)* = The Red Sea]**

The next thing you must do is bring back the following description of Daniel 7:17 below,

[The four great beasts are four kingdoms that will rise from the earth]

(Note5: There is a major clue revealed by this description. For example: Each of the four kingdoms has a material element associated with it (However, the four kingdoms do not represent the material elements that are associated with them). Each material element is symbolic and reveals a historical revelation that is associated with them. To uncover the clue, you must first start by looking closely at the following descriptions of Daniel 2:38-40)

Look closely at the bold portion in the description of Daniel 2:38-40 below,

[**You, O king, are the king of kings, to whom the God of heaven has given the kingdom**, the power, the strength and the glory; and wherever the sons of men dwell, or the beasts of the field, or the birds of the sky, He has given them into your hand and has caused you to rule over them all. You are the head of gold. "**After you there will arise another kingdom inferior to you, then another third kingdom of bronze, which will rule over all the earth. Then there will be a fourth kingdom as strong as iron**; for iron breaks and smashes everything--and as iron breaks things to pieces, so it will crush and break all the others]

Next, remove only the material elements from the descriptions as seen below,

1- **1st kingdom = Element of Gold**
2- **2nd kingdom = ?**
3- **3rd kingdom = Element of Bronze**
4- **4th kingdom = Element of Iron**

(Note6: If you look closely at the above descriptions, you will notice a missing material element (not associated with the 2nd kingdom). However, this is easy to understand as was previously revealed in the early chapters. For example: The unknown element of the 2nd kingdom (will rise inferior to the element of Gold), represents the element of Silver))

Next, re-list the four kingdoms and merge the missing element of Silver with its respective kingdom,

1- 1st kingdom = **Element of Gold**
2- 2nd kingdom = **Element of Silver**
3- 3rd kingdom = **Element of Bronze**
4- 4th kingdom = **Element of Iron**

(Note7: If you look closely at the elements, you will discover they correspond to periods of fallen dynasties. For example: These elements represent the following dynasties: Egypt, Babylon, Assyria, Persia, Nubia, and Greece)

Next, re-list the following elements and place them in the correct places in association with the periods of Ages referring to the dynasties.

1- 1st kingdom = Element of Gold = [**Age of the Egyptian Empire**]
2- 2nd kingdom = Element of Silver = [**Age of the Babylonian and Assyrian Empire's**]
3- 3rd kingdom = Element of Bronze = [**Age of the Persian and Nubian Empire's**]
4- 4th kingdom = Element of Iron = [**Age of the Greek Empire**]

(Note8: The Nation of Judah (element of clay), conquered by the Empire of Babylon, and the Kingdom of Samaria (element of clay) conquered by the Assyrian Empire, went into exile in the Age of silver. Therefore, the Empires of Babylon and Assyria ushered in the element of silver. The Babylonian Empire and the Assyrian Empire (element of silver) trumps the element of clay; but will remain inferior to the land, Wadi of Egypt (ushers in the element of gold). The Egyptian dynasty fell by the rise of the Kushite Empire, known as the Empire of Nubia, who ruled the land of Egypt during the 25th dynasty (thus, the element of gold trumps the elements of clay and silver). This revelation corresponds to the following description 'At that time gifts will be brought to the LORD Almighty from a people tall and smooth-skinned, from a people feared far and wide, an aggressive nation of strange speech, whose land is divided by rivers' – Isaiah 18:7. The rise of the Persian Empire and the rise of the Nubian Empire (ushers in the element of bronze), who conquered the Babylonian and the Assyrian Empire's and remained a powerful force throughout the regions reveals the meaning behind the following description 'which will rule over all the earth' – Daniel 2:39 (thus, the element of bronze trumps the elements of clay, gold and silver). Finally, the rise of the Greek Empire (ushers in the element of Iron), would later rise to conquer the Persian Empire and would itself extend its power all the way to parts of Africa referring to the eastern region of Egypt (region land of Put). This revelation reveals the meaning behind the following description 'for iron breaks and smashes everything--and as iron breaks things to pieces, so it will crush and break all the others' – Daniel 2:40 (thus, the element of Iron trumps the elements of clay, gold, silver, and bronze))

The next thing you must do is bring back the base decoder and merge the elements with their corresponding dynasty in the correct places as seen below,

- {1ST prominent horn} = [4TH head = 4TH hill = 4TH king] = [4th star = 4th spirit before his throne = 4th angel blasting 4th trumpet] = [4th priest *(blowing trumpet)* = Harps = 4th man = 4th elder of Judah = 4th golden lampstand] = [1ST beast = lion = 1ST living creature = like a lion = 1ST cherubim = 1ST chariot = Brown horses = 1ST spirit = 1ST angel = North = 1st wind of the earth = 1st wind of heaven *(churning up the great sea)* = 1ST guard of the city = 1ST apocalyptic rider *(Its rider held a bow)* = Brown horses = 1ST swift messenger = Peals of thunder] = [1ST kingdom = **Element of Gold = Fall of the Egyptian dynasty**]

- {2ND prominent horn} = [5TH head = 5TH hill = 5TH king] = [5th star = 5th spirit before his throne = 5th angel blasting 5th trumpet] = [5th priest *(blowing trumpet)* = cymbals = 5th man = 5th elder of Judah = 5th golden lampstand] = [2ND beast = bear = 2ND living creature = like an ox = 2ND cherubim = 2ND chariot = Black horses = 2ND spirit = 2ND angel = South = 2nd wind of the earth = 2nd wind of heaven *(churning up the great sea)* = 2ND guard of the city = 2ND apocalyptic rider *(Its rider was holding a pair of scales in his hand)* = Black horses = 2ND swift messenger = Rumblings] = [2ND kingdom = **Element of Silver = Fall of the Babylonian and Assyrian dynasties**]

- {3RD prominent horn} = [6TH head = 6TH hill = 6TH king] = [6th star = 6th spirit before his throne = 6th angel blasting 6th trumpet] = [6th priest *(blowing trumpet)* = Lyres = 6th man = 6th elder of Judah = 6th golden lampstand] = [3RD beast = leopard = 3RD living creature = face like a man = 3RD cherubim = 3RD chariot = Pale horses = 3RD spirit = 3RD angel = West = 3rd wind of the earth = 3rd wind of heaven *(churning up the great sea)* = 3RD guard of the city = 3RD apocalyptic rider *(to kill by sword, famine and plague)* = Pale horses = 3RD swift messenger = Flashes of lightning] = [3RD kingdom = **Element of Bronze = Fall of the Persian and Nubian dynasties**]

- {4ᵀᴴ prominent horn} = [7ᵀᴴ head = 7ᵀᴴ hill = 7ᵀᴴ king *(And he was given a great sword)*] = [7ᵗʰ star = 7ᵗʰ spirit before his throne = 7ᵗʰ angel blasting 7ᵗʰ trumpet] = [7ᵗʰ priest *(blowing trumpet)* = shouts = 7ᵗʰ man = 7ᵗʰ elder of Judah = 7ᵗʰ golden lampstand] = [4ᵀᴴ beast *(The beast and the ten horns you saw)* = Beast coming out of the sea *(ancient serpent)* = Scarlet beast *(devil)* = Red dragon *(Satan)*] = [Satan *(name of a man)* = Mighty angel *(coming up from the east)* = *Who is worthy to break the seals and open the scroll?* 4ᵀᴴ living creature = like a flying eagle = 4ᵀᴴ cherubim = 4ᵀᴴ chariot = Fiery red horses = 4ᵀᴴ spirit = 4ᵀᴴ angel = East = 4ᵗʰ wind of the earth = 4ᵗʰ wind of heaven *(churning up the great sea)* = 4ᵀᴴ guard of the city = 4ᵀᴴ apocalyptic rider *(To him was given a large sword)* = Fiery red horses = 4ᵀᴴ swift messenger = Earthquake] = [Then I saw the beast and the kings of the earth and their armies gathered together to make war against the rider on the horse and his army] = [4ᵗʰ kingdom = **Element of Iron = Fall of the Greek dynasty**]

The next thing you must do is bring back the following description of Daniel 2:44 and look closely at the bolded portion below,

> [In the time of those kings, **the God of heaven will set up a kingdom that will never be destroyed, nor will it be left to another people.** It will crush all those kingdoms and bring them to an end, but it will itself endure forever]

(Note9: To understand the mystery of this, you will first need to return the description 1st Kings 11:34-36, because hidden within lies a clue that is unforeseen from view)

Next, bring back the description of 1st Kings 11:34-36 and look again at the bold portion of the description.

> [But I will take the whole kingdom out of Solomon's hand; I have made him ruler all the days of his life for the sake of David my servant, whom I chose and who observed my commands and statutes. **I will take the kingdom from his son's hands and give you ten tribes. I will give one tribe to his son** so that David my servant may always have a lamp before me in Jerusalem, the city where I chose to put my name]

(Note10: There are four vital clues hidden within the bolded portion of this description. To reveal the first clue, you must again, separate the beast apart from its ten horns; then merge their respective tribes in place)

To reveal the first clue, look closely at the bold portion of the two illustrations below,

- {Ten Horns} = [Ten kings = Ten tribes = *I will take the kingdom from his son's hands and give you ten tribes* = **Tribes of Ephraim, Manasseh, Naphtali, Dan, Asher, Issachar, Zebulon, Simeon, Reuben, and Gad** = Jeroboam king of Ephraim = Nation of Ephraim = *who are yet to receive a kingdom of their own* = Kingdom of Samaria]

- {Beast} = [single tribe = *I will give one tribe to his son* = **Tribe of Benjamin** = *remained in the city* = Nation of Judah = Rehoboam king of Judah Kingdom of Jerusalem]

The second clue is revealed behind the total sum of the calculation regarding the tribes allotted to the following kings (King Jeroboam) and (King Rehoboam) as revealed in the illustration below,

[Ten tribes *(allotted to King Jeroboam)***]** **(+)** **[Single tribe** *(allotted to King Rehoboam)***]** = **{Eleven tribes}**

(Note11: When viewing the total sum of the calculated tribes allotted to both kings (as representing eleven tribes in all), here you will discover there is a missing twelfth tribe (not allotted to either of the two kings))

The third clue is revealed by bringing back the following description of Daniel 8:9 and look closely at the bold description as seen below,

Daniel 8:9 - [Out of one of them came another horn, **which started small but grew in power to the south and to the east and toward the Beautiful Land**]

(Note12: The bold description is symbolic and corresponds to the missing twelfth tribe. Thus, this tribe will start off small but will grow to great power. Therefore, this tribe will also emerge from within the 4th kingdom))

To reveal the 3rd clue, you must bring back the following revelations revealed by the four prominent horns and merge the bold description of Daniel 8:9 with the 4th prominent horn as representing a 4th kingdom.

$\{1^{ST}$ prominent horn$\}$ = [4TH head = 4TH hill = 4TH king] = [1ST beast = lion = 1ST kingdom]

$\{2^{ND}$ prominent horn$\}$ = [5TH head = 5TH hill = 5TH king] = [2ND beast = bear = 2ND kingdom]

$\{3^{RD}$ prominent horn$\}$ = [6TH head = 6TH hill = 6TH king] = [3RD beast = leopard = 3RD kingdom]

- $\{4^{TH}$ prominent horn *(Out of one of them came another horn)*$\}$ = [7TH head = 7TH hill = 7TH king] = [4TH beast and Ten horns *(there before me was another horn, a little one, which came up among them)* = 4TH kingdom **(started small but grew in power to the south and to the east and toward the Beautiful Land)**]

*(Note13: Within the 4th kingdom reveals a little mysterious tribe that will emerge from within. For example: The **beast** (single tribe) and its **ten horns** (ten tribes) represents a 4th kingdom. The missing twelfth tribe will emerge from within the ten tribes (as representing the ten horns). This revelation corresponds to the following description 'While I was thinking about the horns, there before me was another horn, a little one, which came up among them'. Here lies the paradox. On one hand, the 8th king will emerge from the 4th beast's ten horns. On the other, the missing tribe will emerge from the 4th beast's ten horns as also representing ten tribes, in the same way that the 8th king will emerge from its ten horns (Thus, the ten horns as representing ten kings also represent ten tribes). Therefore, the following description 'While I was thinking about the horns, there before me was another horn, a little one, which came up among them' (as representing the emergence of the 8th king), also corresponds to this description* **'started small but grew in power to the south and to the east and toward the Beautiful Land'** *(as representing the emergence of the missing tribe))*

Here is the [3rd vital clue]: The 5th prominent horn corresponds to an 8th king and represents the following tribe: [Twelfth tribe of Israel].

This revelation is revealed by the following illustration:

$\{5^{TH}$ prominent horn = 5th Beast = 8th King$\}$

- $\{4^{TH}$ prominent horn *(Out of one of them came another horn)*$\}$ = [7TH head = 7TH hill = 7TH king] = [4TH beast = ? = Ten horns *(there before me was another horn, a little one, which came up among them)* = 4TH kingdom **(started small but grew in power to the south and to the east and toward the Beautiful Land)**]

Twelfth Tribe of Israel

The next thing you must do is merge the revelations together regarding the 5th prominent horn in the correct places. *See below,*

- [5th prominent horn] = [Solid gold lampstand = Someone like a son of man = Man clothed in linen (writing kit at his side) = *He came and took the scroll from the right hand of him who sat on the throne!* = *The armies of heaven were following him, riding on white horses and dressed in fine linen, white and clean* = *(And from His mouth proceeds a sharp sword)* = 8th king = King of Kings = Lord of Lords = Naphtali] = [5th beast = Woman = 5th living creature = Lamb looking as if slain *(will hate the prostitute)* = 5th cherubim = 5th chariot = 5th spirit = 5th angel = 5th guard of the city = 5th apocalyptic rider *(from His mouth proceeds a sharp sword)* = A great hailstorm] = [**twelfth tribe** = *started small but grew in power*]

The next thing you must do is look closely at the bold portion in the following description of Daniel 2:44

[In the time of those kings, **the God of heaven will set up a kingdom that will never be destroyed, nor will it be left to another people**. It will crush all those kingdoms and bring them to an end, but it will itself endure forever]

(Note14: *The 4th kingdom (as representing a divided kingdom) corresponds to the following two nations: Judah (single tribe) and Samaria (ten tribes). Thus, it is from the kingdom of Samaria (ten tribes) that a mysterious twelfth tribe will emerge. This twelfth tribe will also emerge into a kingdom that will surpass the 4th kingdom of Iron. This revelation will reveal the meaning behind the description 'It will crush all those kingdoms and bring them to an end'. This revelation corresponds to the following description* **'which started small but grew in power'**)

(Note15: *The* ***four horns*** *that replaced the one that was broken off represent* ***four kingdoms*** *- Daniel 8:22. The* ***four great beasts*** *are* ***four kingdoms*** *that will rise from the earth - Daniel 7:17. The mysterious little horn that emerges from the 4th prominent horn as representing a 5th prominent horn, as well as a 5th beast, will also come to represent a kingdom as well, just like the others*)

Here is the [**4th vital clue**]: The **5th prominent horn,** as representing the **5th beast** corresponds to the **twelfth tribe** and represents the following kingdom: [5th Kingdom].

The next thing you must do is merge the revelations together regarding the 5th prominent horn in the correct place.

- [5th prominent horn] = [Solid gold lampstand = Someone like a son of man = Man clothed in linen (writing kit at his side) = *He came and took the scroll from the right hand of him who sat on the throne!* = *The armies of heaven were following him, riding on white horses and dressed in fine linen, white and clean* = *(And from His mouth proceeds a sharp sword)* = 8th king = King of Kings = Lord of Lords = Naphtali] = [5th beast = Woman = 5th living creature = Lamb looking as if slain *(will hate the prostitute)* = 5th cherubim = 5th chariot = 5th spirit = 5th angel = 5th guard of the city = 5th apocalyptic rider *(from His mouth proceeds a sharp sword)* = A great hailstorm] = [twelfth tribe = *started small but grew in power* = **5th Kingdom**]

(Note16: Like the four Kingdoms, and their associated elements as representing periods of fallen dynasties, this 5th Kingdom also has an element that is associated with it. However, it represents an era that has not yet emerged. This element will serve as a symbol that will come to represent the surpassing of the Age of Iron. To locate the next clue, you must look closely at the description of Daniel 2:45)

Look closely at the bold portion in the description of Daniel 2:45 below,

> [**This is the meaning of the vision of the rock cut out of a mountain,** but not by human hands--a rock that broke the iron, the bronze, the clay, the silver and the gold to pieces. "God has shown the king what will take place in the future. The dream is true and its interpretation is trustworthy]

Next, re-list the 5th kingdom and merge the associated element as seen below,

5- 5th kingdom = **Element of Rock**

(Note17: The 5th kingdom of Rock is symbolic and represents a coming Age that will surpass the Age of Iron. Thus, the element of rock trumps the elements of clay, gold, silver, bronze and iron. This revelation corresponds to the following description **'a rock that broke the iron, the bronze, the clay, the silver and the gold to pieces'** *– Daniel 2:45)*

(Note18: The second part of the description regarding Daniel 2:45, reveals the clue as to what the element of Rock will symbolize. For example: look closely at what the description says, **'"God has shown the king what will take place in the future'**. *This description* **"in the future"** *reveals the rise of a coming Age that will emerge to bring about the fall of the Age of Iron)*

Next, re-list the element of rock and merge the associated Age as seen below,

- 5th kingdom = Element of Rock = **Coming Age**

The next thing you must do is bring back the base decoder and merge the element with its corresponding era in the correct place as seen below,

- [5th prominent horn] = [Solid gold lampstand = Someone like a son of man = Man clothed in linen (writing kit at his side) = *He came and took the scroll from the right hand of him who sat on the throne! = The armies of heaven were following him, riding on white horses and dressed in fine linen, white and clean = (And from His mouth proceeds a sharp sword)* = 8th king = King of Kings = Lord of Lords = Naphtali] = [5th beast = Woman = 5th living creature = Lamb looking as if slain *(will hate the prostitute)* = 5th cherubim = 5th chariot = White horses = 5th spirit = 5th angel = 5th guard of the city = 5th apocalyptic rider *(from His mouth proceeds a sharp sword)* = White horses = A great hailstorm] = [twelfth tribe = *started small but grew in power* = 5th kingdom = **Element of Rock = Coming Age**]

The next thing you must do is look closely at the bold portion in the following description of Revelation 17:15.

[Then the angel said to me, "**The waters you saw, where the prostitute sits, are peoples, multitudes, nations and languages**]

*(Note19: Within this description reveals another major clue. For example: This description 'The waters you saw, where the prostitute sits' corresponds to the following description 'One of them said to the man clothed in linen, who was above the waters of the river' – Daniel 12:6. Therefore, the **'prostitute'** (waters you saw, where the prostitute sits) and the **'man clothed in linen'** (who was above the waters of the river) both corresponds to the description **'someone like a son of man'**))*

Here is the revelation: A 5th beast, as representing a Woman, rose above the water of the Red Sea, which overlooks the Blue and White Nile Rivers, after being churned up by the four winds of heaven, as representing four winds of the earth.

What is the name of the woman depicted as the prostitute?

To answer this question, you must start by bringing back the following revelation regarding the (ten horns) and the (beast), and look closely at the tribes as seen below,

- {Ten Horns} = [Ten kings = Ten tribes = *I will take the kingdom from his son's hands and give you ten tribes* = **Tribes of Ephraim, Manasseh, Naphtali, Dan, Asher, Issachar, Zebulon, Simeon, Reuben, and Gad** = Jeroboam king of Ephraim = Nation of Ephraim = *who are yet to receive a kingdom of their own* Nation of Ephraim = *who are yet to receive a kingdom of their own* = Kingdom of Samaria]

- {Beast} = [single tribe = *I will give one tribe to his son* = **Tribe of Benjamin** = *remained in the city* = Nation of Judah = Rehoboam king of Judah]

(Note20: As revealed previously, Judah does not represent a tribe of Israel; but represents a nation born from the tribe of Benjamin. If you look closely at the numbers of listed tribes below, you will discover that Jacob produced twelve descendants, not eleven (Thus, there are only eleven tribes revealed by the description **'I will take the kingdom from his son's hands and give you ten tribes. I will give one tribe to his son so that David my servant may always have a lamp before me'** *– 1ˢᵗ Kings 11:34-36). There is a revealing clue hidden behind the mystery regarding Jacob's twelfth descendant)*

Next, bring back the following descriptions of Revelation 7:5-8

1- [From the tribes of *Reuben* 12,000 were sealed]
2- [From the tribes of *Gad* 12,000 were sealed]
3- [From the tribes of *Asher* 12,000 were sealed]
4- [From the tribes of *Naphtali* 12,000 were sealed]
5- [From the tribes of *Manasseh* 12,000 were sealed]
6- [From the tribe of *Simeon* 12,000 were sealed]
7- [From the tribe of *Levi* 12,000 were sealed]
8- [From the tribe of *Issachar* 12,000 were sealed]
9- [From the tribe of *Zebulon* 12,000 were sealed]
10- [From the tribe of *Joseph* 12,000 were sealed]
11- [From the tribe of *Benjamin* 12,000 were sealed]

Here is the next clue: The name of **Jacob's twelfth descendant** corresponds to the name of the missing **twelfth tribe of Israel** and represents the name of the following tribe: [The tribe of Dinah]!

Next, bring back the following descriptions and merge the tribe of Dinah in place of the tribe of Judah.

1- **[From the tribe of *Dinah* 12,000 were sealed]**
2- [From the tribes of *Reuben* 12,000 were sealed]
3- [From the tribes of *Gad* 12,000 were sealed]
4- [From the tribes of *Asher* 12,000 were sealed]
5- [From the tribes of *Naphtali* 12,000 were sealed]
6- [From the tribes of *Manasseh* 12,000 were sealed]
7- [From the tribe of *Simeon* 12,000 were sealed]
8- [From the tribe of *Levi* 12,000 were sealed]
9- [From the tribe of *Issachar* 12,000 were sealed]
10- [From the tribe of *Zebulon* 12,000 were sealed]
11- [From the tribe of *Joseph* 12,000 were sealed]
12- [From the tribe of *Benjamin* 12,000 were sealed]

*(Note21: The word **'prostitute'** is symbolic and corresponds to the description 'someone like a son of man' and represents the name of Jacob's twelfth descendant, known as 'Dinah'. The word **'prostitute'** corresponds to the word **'defiled'** (thus, Dinah was defiled). This revelation corresponds to this description 'Now Dinah, the daughter Leah had borne to Jacob, went out to visit the women of the land. When Shechem son of Hamor the Hivite, the ruler of that area, saw her, he took her and raped her.' – Genesis 34:1-2. This revelation will be revealed in more detail momentarily. The defiling of Dinah represents the violent sexual rape of Dinah and corresponds to the following description **'But they replied, "Should he have treated our sister like a prostitute?' – Genesis 34:31.** The manner, in which Shechem defiled Dinah reveals the meaning behind this description **'Then I saw a Lamb, looking as if it had been slain.'** – Revelation 5:6)*

The next thing you must do is bring back the base decoder regarding the 5th prominent horn and merge the revelation together in the correct places.

- [5th prominent horn] = [Solid gold lampstand = Someone like a son of man = Man clothed in linen (writing kit at his side) = *He came and took the scroll from the right hand of him who sat on the throne! = The armies of heaven were following him, riding on white horses and dressed in fine linen, white and clean* = *(And from His mouth proceeds a sharp sword)* = 8th king = King of Kings = Lord of Lords = Naphtali] = [5th beast = Woman = **Dinah** = 5th living creature = Lamb looking as if slain *(will hate the prostitute)* = 5th cherubim = 5th chariot = White horses = 5th spirit = 5th angel = 5th guard of the city = 5th apocalyptic rider *(from His mouth proceeds a sharp sword)* = White horses = A great hailstorm] = [twelfth tribe = **The tribe of Dinah** = *started small but grew in power* = 5th kingdom = Element of Rock = Coming Age]

Look closely at the following description of Matthew 12:42 below,

[The Queen of the South will rise at the judgment with this generation and condemn it; for she came from the ends of the earth]

*(Note22: Within this description reveals a hidden clue. For example: **Dinah** is also symbolic and corresponds to the description 'the waters you saw where the prostitute sits.' The prostitute is also symbolic and corresponds to the Queen of the South. Thus, the waters where the prostitute sits (as referring to the Red Sea) is in the land of the south, the land of Egypt. The **Queen of the South** (as also referring to the land of Egypt) is also symbolic and corresponds to the description 'a woman clothed with the sun'. Here lies the unseen revelation. When you look at the following revelation: (Dinah = prostitute = Queen of the South = a woman clothed with the sun), you will discover its beginning to reveal the revelation of the 5th **spirit of heaven**. As revealed previously, the four great beasts churning up the great sea corresponds to the four spirits of heaven as representing the four winds of the earth, which are churning up the Red Sea. Thus, they are churning up the 5th beast who represents the 5th spirit of heaven. The 5th spirit does not correspond to a wind of the earth like the others but corresponds to the great star of the earth that appears over the waters of the Red Sea. This description 'for she came from the ends of the earth' is symbolic and corresponds to the 5th spirit of heaven that represents the great star of the earth that journeys across the sky from the north to the land of the south (thus, during the end of a particular period referring to the summer solstice, the great star of the earth will journey from the north to the south and will appear at its highest point in the southern hemisphere over the Red Sea in the land of Egypt). This revelation will also be revealed in more detail in the 2nd Chronicle's titled 'The Elijah Doctrine2 (The Path of the Sign))*

Here is the next clue: The **5th spirit of heaven** *(churned up over the Red Sea)* represents the following great star of heaven: [The Sun]!

The next thing you must do is bring back the base decoder regarding the 5th prominent horn and merge the revelation together in the correct place.

- [5th prominent horn] = [Solid gold lampstand = Someone like a son of man = Man clothed in linen (writing kit at his side) = *He came and took the scroll from the right hand of him who sat on the throne! = The armies of heaven were following him, riding on white horses and dressed in fine linen, white and clean = (And from His mouth proceeds a sharp sword)* = 8th king = King of Kings = Lord of Lords = Naphtali] = [5th beast = Woman = Dinah = 5th living creature = Lamb looking as if slain *(will hate the prostitute)* = 5th cherubim = 5th chariot = White horses = 5th spirit = **The Sun** = 5th angel = 5th guard of the city = 5th apocalyptic rider *(from His mouth proceeds a sharp sword)* = White horses = A great hailstorm] = [twelfth tribe = The tribe of Dinah = *started small but grew in power* = 5th kingdom = Element of Rock = Coming Age]

The next thing you must do is look closely at the bold description of Revelation 12:1.

[A great and wondrous sign appeared in heaven; a woman clothed with the sun, with the moon under her feet and a crown of twelve stars on her head]

*(Note23: Within this description reveals another major clue. For example: The **woman clothed with the sun** is symbolic and corresponds to the description **'the waters you saw where the prostitute sits'** – Revelation 17:15, as also corresponding to the **Queen of the south** as representing the 5th **spirit** as the **Sun**))*

*(Note24: This description **'A great and wondrous sign'** is also symbolic and corresponds to an astronomical phenomenon that takes place in the land of Egypt every year and will symbolize the end of the summer solstice, which will end in the southern hemisphere. However, the birth of this sign (not referring to it's surpassing) will be revealed in more detail in the 2nd Chronicle's titled 'The Elijah Doctrine2 (The Path of the Sign))*

Here is the next clue: The description '**A great and wondrous sign**' corresponds to the **Sun** and represents the passing of the following sign that will appear over the waters of the Red Sea: [**The passing of the Sign of Jonah**]!

*(Note25: The passing of the Sign of Jonah reveals a vital clue that will begin to reveal the very mystery of God. This mystery corresponds to the name of an astronomical event that occurs once every year in the land of Egypt! This revelation will correspond to this description **'the star they had seen in the east went ahead of them until it stopped over the place where the child was'** – Matthew 2:9. This revelation will also be revealed in more detail in the 2nd Chronicles of the Elijah Doctrine)*

Here is the final revelation: The **passing of the Sign of Jonah** corresponds to the **great and wonderous sign** as corresponding to an astronomical phenomenon that occurs in the land of Egypt: [The end of the summer solstice]!

(Note26: The end of the summer solstice (as representing the passing of the Sign of Jonah) occurs on December 21st, in which the Sun's path becomes a little higher in the southern hemisphere. Thus, on December 21st the sun will stop along the equator, in the tropic of Capricorn (summer will end in the southern hemisphere). It is here, where the solstice will reverse, rise again, and set towards the direction where there would be sunrise. This revelation will also be revealed in more detail in the 2nd Chronicles of the Elijah Doctrine))

The next thing you must do is bring back the base decoder regarding the 5th prominent horn and merge the revelations regarding the Sun *(falls to the land of the South)* with the corresponding land regarding the Solstice change *(The Kushite land of Egypt)* into the correct places.

- [5th prominent horn] = [Solid gold lampstand = Someone like a son of man = Man clothed in linen (writing kit at his side) = *He came and took the scroll from the right hand of him who sat on the throne! = The armies of heaven were following him, riding on white horses and dressed in fine linen, white and clean =* (*And from His mouth proceeds a sharp sword*) = 8th king = King of Kings = Lord of Lords = Naphtali] = [5th beast = Woman = Dinah = 5th living creature = Lamb looking as if slain *(will hate the prostitute)* = 5th cherubim = 5th chariot = White horses = 5th angel = 5th guard of the city = 5th apocalyptic rider *(from His mouth proceeds a sharp sword)* = White horses = A great hailstorm] = [twelfth tribe = The tribe of Dinah = *started small but grew in power* = 5th kingdom = Element of Rock = Coming Age] = {Pharaoh Tirhakah *(Pharoah of Egypt)*} = [Empire of Kush] = [Land divided by rivers: *(Blue Nile River)* and *(White Nile River)*] = [a people tall and smooth-skinned, to a people feared far and wide, an aggressive nation of strange speech] = [Invaded the land of Egypt *(Egypt fell in the 25th dynasty)*] = [Invaded the land of Assyria *(captured the Samarian Israelites)*] = [Ancient Nubia *(land of the Kushites)*] = [Western region of upper Egypt = Punt *(Libyans)*] and [Eastern region of upper Egypt = Put *(Nubians)* = **The Red Sea** *(waters you saw where the prostitute sits)*] = [**Queen of the South** *(Woman clothed with the sun)* = **A great and wondrous sign = 5th spirit = The Sun = The passing of the Sign of Jonah** *(summer solstice ends in the southern hemisphere)* = **End of the Summer Solstice** *(on Dec 21st)*]

THE 7TH ANGEL'S TRUMPET

The next thing you must do is look closely at the bold portion of the description in Revelation 10:7.

> [**But in the days when the seventh angel is about to sound his trumpet**, the mystery of God will be accomplished, just as he announced to his servants the prophets]

To uncover the mystery of the true sounding blast of the 7th angel's trumpet, you must bring back the following description revealed in the book of 1ST Chronicles 15:28. See below,

> [So all Israel brought up the ark of the covenant of the Lord with shouts, with the sounding of rams,' horns and trumpets, and of cymbals, and the playing of lyres and Harps]

(Note27: The 7th angel's trumpet blast – Revelation 10:7, corresponds to the 7th priest trumpet blast - 1ST Chronicles 15:24. This revelation corresponds to the following description – 'Shebaniah, Joshaphat, Nethanel, Amasai, Zechariah, Benaiah and Eliezer the priests were to blow trumpets before the ark of God')

To sound the trumpet, bring back the following revelation revealed by the base decoder regarding the 7th angel and merge the 'sound' corresponding to the 7th priest.

Listen closely as the 7th priest, representing the 7th angel reveal the sounding blast of his trumpet as seen below,

- {4TH prominent horn} = [7TH head = 7TH hill = 7TH king *(And he was given a great sword)*] = [7th star = 7th spirit before his throne = **7th angel blasting 7th trumpet = 7th priest *(blowing trumpet)* = shouts**] = [7th man = 7th elder of Judah = 7th golden lampstand] = [4TH beast *(The beast and the ten horns you saw)* = Beast coming out of the sea *(ancient serpent)* = Scarlet beast *(devil)* = Red dragon *(Satan)*] = [Satan *(name of a man)* = Mighty angel *(coming up from the east)* = Who is worthy to break the seals and open the scroll? 4TH living creature = like a flying eagle = 4TH cherubim = 4TH chariot = Fiery red horses = 4TH spirit = 4TH angel = East = 4th wind of the earth = 4th wind of heaven *(churning up the great sea)* = 4TH guard of the city = 4TH apocalyptic rider *(To him was given a large sword)* = Fiery red horses =

4TH swift messenger = Earthquake] = [Then I saw the beast and the kings of the earth and their armies gathered together to make war against the rider on the horse and his army] = [4th kingdom = Element of Iron = Fall of the Greek Empire]

Here is the next clue: The **7th angel sounding his trumpet** correspond to the **7th priest blasting his trumpet** and represents the following sound of the trumpet blast: [the sound of 'shouts']

{Important note. There is an important revelation soon to be revealed regarding the mystery of why the 7th trumpet blast corresponds to the sound of 'shouts' that will be revealed in detail very shortly}

The next thing you must do is look closely at the description of Genesis 34:1-2 below,

[Now Dinah, the daughter Leah had borne to Jacob, went out to visit the women of the land. When Shechem son of Hamor the Hivite, the ruler of that area, saw her, he took her and raped her]

(Note28: There is a hidden clue revealed by this description. For example: The Queen of the South (came from the ends of the earth), who rises above the waters of the Red Sea (as representing the woman clothed with the sun), corresponds to the only daughter born to Jacob who had been defiled (the waters you saw where the prostitute sits). Thus, Dinah represents the virgin daughter born to Jacob who was raped by the son of Hamar the Hivite (as representing the Lamb looking as if slain). This revelation corresponds to the following description **'Meanwhile, Jacob's sons had come in from the fields as soon as they heard what had happened. They were shocked and furious, because Shechem had done an outrageous thing in Israel by sleeping with Jacob's daughter--a thing that should not be done' – Genesis 34:7.** *To reveal the clue, you must look closely at the description of Isaiah 7:14)*

Look closely at the description of Isaiah 7:14 below,

> [Therefore the Lord himself will give you a sign: The virgin will conceive and give birth to a son, and will call him Immanuel]

(Note29: The virgin in this description does not correspond to Mary, as some Scholars will have you believe. The understanding of this will be revealed in broader detail in the 2nd Chronicle titled, The Elijah Doctrine2 (The Path of the Sign). On the contrary, the virgin in this description corresponds to Dinah, the virgin daughter of Jacob. When Shechem had sexual relations with Dinah he did so by force. Because of his actions Dinah conceived before she was removed from his house. This revelation corresponds to the description – 'When a man has sexual relations with a woman and there is an emission of semen, both of them must bathe with water' – Leviticus 15:18. This revelation reveals the meaning behind the description 'They put Hamor and his son Shechem to the sword and took Dinah from Shechem's house and left' – Genesis 34:26. This revelation corresponds to the blasting of the seventh trumpet (the very moment before the mystery of God will be revealed))

Here is the final revelation: The **sounding of the 7th angel's trumpet** *(the Lord himself will give you a sign)* corresponds to the sounding blast of **'shouts'** and represents the following revelation: [On December 21st, in the Kushite land of Egypt, when the sun stops along the equator in the tropic of Capricorn, marking the end of the summer solstice, the sign of Jonah will pass, and summer will end in the southern hemisphere. And in that moment, Dinah the lamb looking as if slain, will give birth to another sign that will appear over the waters of the Red Sea, and the Samarian exiles, that were exiled to the land of the Wadi of Egypt, will call it Immanuel]!

(Note30: The Queen of the South (woman clothed with the sun) as corresponding to Jacob's daughter Dinah (waters you saw where the prostitute sits) also corresponds to the following description **'The virgin will conceive and give birth to a son'** *- Isaiah 7:14. This revelation is also symbolic and corresponds to the passing of the Sign of Jonah, in which the summer solstice will draw near to its end in the southern hemisphere on December 21st. Thus, a new solstice and sign will be born in the Kushite land of Egypt, and the Samarians exiles will call the phenomenon Immanuel. And so, the sounding blast of* **'shouts'** *is symbolic and corresponds to the labor pains of Dinah's approaching delivery. This revelation corresponds to the following description* **'As a pregnant woman about to give birth writhes and cries out in her pain'** –

Isaiah 26:17. Dinah's approaching delivery will symbolize the birth of the solstice change, which will be born on the day of December 21st. This revelation reveals the meaning behind this description **'She was pregnant and cried out in pain as she was about to give birth. Then another sign appeared in heaven'** – *Revelation 12:2-3. The sign corresponding to the next solstice change will be revealed in more detail within the 2nd Chronicle titled: The Elijah Doctrine2 (The Path of the Sign))*

Congratulations! You have successfully completed the 4th Chapter, by revealing the true revelation behind the Lamb looking as though slain!

{**Important note:** The second part of the revelation as described in the verse of Revelation 10:7 - **'the mystery of God will be accomplished, just as he announced to his servants the prophets'** will be revealed in full detail within the 2nd Chronicle titled, 'The Elijah Doctrine2' (The Path of the Sign)}

You have proven yourself worthy of possessing the first piece of the Grail map. Complete your journey by proceeding to the final page!

Here is the [1ˢᵗ map coordinates to the ancient city]:

{Start - **[North]** - of the compass line -do- **[South]** – and journey to the eastern region of Egypt, revealed previously as the ancient region Put *(land of the Nubians)*}

Congratulations! You have successfully completed the 1ˢᵗ Cryptex puzzle!

The Elijah Doctrine Chronicles is dedicated to:

My daughters: Yahanna T. Bennett, Elayah P. Bennett and Saharah A. Bennett

My Mother: Olivia Bennett

Special dedication:

To all the free thinkers of the world; past and present!

'We will end this war and redeem the souls of the damned and the lives of the condemned! Together, we will raise to the surface a new world. A world that stands as one people, nation, and languages under one banner to bring to justice the institutions that have perverted our humanity. You shall be set free from the bondage of others who seek to keep your minds captive to the darkness of ignorance, and you shall awaken to the truth of disillusion!'

Elijah H. Bennett

You may continue to the 2nd Chronicle_ **The Elijah Doctrine2_The Path of the Sign**…

www.ingramcontent.com/pod-product-compliance
Lightning Source LLC
Chambersburg PA
CBHW080505110426
42742CB00017B/3004